MW00579165

Power Forward

Power Forward

My Journey from Illiterate NBA Player to a Magna Cum Laude Master's Degree

Dean Tolson

with Lindsay Harrison

Essex, Connecticut

An imprint of Globe Pequot, the trade division of
The Rowman & Littlefield Publishing Group, Inc.
4501 Forbes Blvd., Ste. 200
Lanham, MD 20706
www.rowman.com

Distributed by NATIONAL BOOK NETWORK

British Library Cataloguing in Publication Information available

Library of Congress Cataloging-in-Publication Data available
Names: Tolson, Dean, 1951- author.
Title: Power forward : my journey from illiterate NBA player to a magna cum laude master's degree / Dean Tolson With Lindsay Harrison.
Description: Essex, Connecticut : Lyons Press, [2023]
Identifiers: LCCN 2023007899 (print) | LCCN 2023007900 (ebook) | ISBN 9781493076895 (cloth) | ISBN 9781493078455 (epub)
Subjects: LCSH: Tolson, Dean, 1951- | Basketball players--United States--Biography. | Illiterate persons--United States--Biography. | Basketball--Kansas--Kansas City--History. | Arkansas Razorbacks (Basketball team)--History. | Seattle SuperSonics (Basketball team)–History
Classification: LCC GV884.T63 A3 2023 (print) | LCC GV884.T63 (ebook) | DDC 796.323092 [B]–dc23/eng/20230314
LC record available at https://lccn.loc.gov/2023007899
LC ebook record available at https://lccn.loc.gov/2023007900

∞™ The paper used in this publication meets the minimum requirements of American National Standard for Information Sciences—Permanence of Paper for Printed Library Materials, ANSI/NISO Z39.48-1992.

This book is dedicated to the memory of coach J. Frank Broyles, a man of character, integrity, class, and honesty. He became a born-again Christian and completely went out of his way to help an illiterate record-holding athlete to achieve academic success at the highest level at a Division I university. Coach Broyles was the father figure and mentor I'd never had. He was steadfast in his conviction and promise to me. He said, "Tree, as long as you can make your grades and keep up, I promise the university will pay until the day you graduate, no matter how long it takes. That's my solemn promise." Thank you, Coach Broyles, from the bottom of my heart for allowing me the opportunity to help others. May you rest in peace.

Coach/AD Frank Broyles holding diploma
COURTESY OF *SPORTS ILLUSTRATED*, PHOTOGRAPHER/PHIL HUBER

Contents

Chapter One

With older brother Bobby
COURTESY OF THE AUTHOR

I guess, in a way, my first dream started with a knock at the front door when I was five years old, and I ran to answer it. Daddy had left us by then, so Mother, my older brother Bobby, my grandmother, and I moved from a farm in Bonner Springs, Kansas, to Kansas City, Missouri, to be closer to Mother's two older brothers. Daddy's younger sister, my aunt Eula May Tolson, had become close to Mother, and sometimes she would leave the University of Kansas on weekends to come visit us.

That day Eula May had decided to bring her new boyfriend to meet us.

I still remember opening the door and staring up at that giant man. He was almost as tall as the sky, and I didn't even come up to his knees. Somehow he was graceful, with these huge hands and the biggest smile

Mother, Father, and Grandmother
COURTESY OF THE AUTHOR

I'd ever seen, that he aimed right at Bobby and me as he lowered his head to walk through the door. All of a sudden he grabbed me with one of those big hands, grabbed Bobby with the other, and swung us around like rag dolls. When he finally put us down, we ran away, squealing with laughter, and then snuck back into the living room, hoping he would do it again.

From then on, every weekend, I couldn't wait to see if Eula May and her boyfriend were coming back to visit. When they did, Bobby and I sprinted to play with him. He always seemed so happy to be with us, and it made me feel special that this kind, friendly giant liked spending time with me.

When he and Eula May split up and he stopped coming around, I was sure I'd never see him again. I was wrong.

It was four years later. I was nine years old. Mother was working three jobs, and we were so poor we were just barely getting by, so it was like a miracle when she came home one day with a small black-and-white television, our very first one. She wanted Bobby and me to stay off the streets, where, even if Black kids in Kansas City weren't looking for trouble, trouble had a way of finding them, and that TV was something that might keep us in the house.

I turned it on, and magically, a picture appeared on the screen. A basketball game. I'd never seen one before, and I couldn't take my eyes off it. An announcer said it was the Philadelphia Warriors versus the world champion Boston Celtics . . . and suddenly, in the middle of all those players, there he was! There was Aunt Eula May's boyfriend! The same man who'd swung my brother and me around the living room and made us laugh until we could barely breathe, and laughed as hard as we did, and then set us down so gently to make sure he'd never hurt us. It was him, on TV!

Wilt Chamberlain, they said his name was. A big track star from the University of Kansas, who could run the 100-yard dash in 10.9 seconds, throw a shotput 56 feet, and won the Big Eight high jump championship three years straight! He wasn't just Eula May's boyfriend back then, he was a superhero! Then he left the University of Kansas to join the Harlem

Globetrotters, and a year later he went to play for the Philadelphia Warriors in the NBA. Fans who used to watch college basketball followed him there, as basketball changed forever from a slow, lumbering game to a fast-paced, exciting event. Wilt Chamberlain averaged 50 points a game for an entire season, and the NBA became the place to be.

And now, there he was, running up and down the court among those other giants, battling an incredible player named Bill Russell of the Boston Celtics. Wilt. "The Big Dipper," they called him, leaping and twisting and turning, rolling the ball off his fingers right into the basket, thrilling the cheering, applauding people who were packed into the bleachers going crazy.

From that day on, I knew exactly what I wanted to do with my life. I wanted to play basketball. I wanted to be an NBA star and play on TV like Wilt. It wasn't just something I wanted; it was an intention, almost a destiny. I knew it. How I knew it with such certainty at nine years old is still a mystery, but any doubts I might have had were erased when I touched my first basketball. It felt round, a little heavy, it smelled like cowhide leather, and in some way I can't begin to explain, it felt right. Comfortable. Impossibly familiar, like something I'd been waiting for that I didn't even know existed.

I remember walking back into the house and making the announcement. "Mother," I said, "I'm going to play in the NBA."

She just glanced at me, shook her head, and replied, "You're just like all the rest of them nappy-headed little Black boys who want to do that."

"No, Mother, you don't understand. I'm different. I'm going to do that."

She walked away as if she hadn't heard me. It didn't discourage me at all. In fact, I couldn't wait to prove her wrong. And looking back, I can't blame her for not believing me. I'm sure she had dreams too when she was a child, but they'd died of neglect a long time ago.

Mother gave birth to me in Kansas City, Kansas, on a frigid, snowy Sunday in November of 1951, a year after my brother Bobby was born. Midwestern farmers know that kind of cold, the kind that pierces your body and settles in your bones like a cruel squatter. Then she took me home to our small rural farm in Bonner Springs, Kansas, 20 miles away.

There were two beds in our one-room house. Mother and Daddy slept in one. I slept in the other one with Bobby and our mother's mother, Louise Hayes, our granny. There was a wood-burning stove in the center of the room that kept the house heated in the winter and gave Granny a place to make our meals and warm the water for our baths. Daddy gathered and cut the wood for the stove, and Mother fed the wood into it to keep it burning.

Daddy, Booker Tolson, was a sharecropper from Garnett, Kansas. He was tall for the men of his day, with wavy brown hair, a strong constitution, and caramel skin that bronzed in the sun. He raised chickens, hogs, and cows, and he grew corn and wheat. He was also a self-taught painter and carpenter who did a little bit of everything to provide for the family.

Mother, Melba Tolson, was a beautiful woman from Marshall, Missouri. She was statuesque, 6-foot-1, and always well dressed, with a ready smile and a gentle way, unless she was pushed too far. Then she had no problem pushing back twice as hard, no matter how big and strong you were. She worked the land with Daddy without a single complaint.

My parents met in Kansas City, Missouri, when Mother was visiting her older brothers, my Uncle Raymond and my Uncle Tiken. She was 15 years old. Daddy was 26. Granny didn't like my dad from the very beginning. She thought he was trouble, and she was right. But Mother married him, and they started a family.

Daddy and Mother spent long, hard hours, seven days a week, working on the farm in Bonner Springs, so Granny was pretty much in charge of looking after Bobby and me. She was the strongest, most tireless woman I've ever known—there was no farm work she couldn't handle, including washing all the family clothes on an old wooden washboard with galvanized metal ripples that hung on the side of the tub.

That same tub was where she'd bring hot water from the wood-burning stove and give Bobby and me a bath. We had fun splashing water at each other and all over the floor, and Granny would scold us. "Boys, stop splashing water out of that tub, or I'll spank the both of you." One day, Bobby kept splashing, and I witnessed his first spanking. Thankfully, I

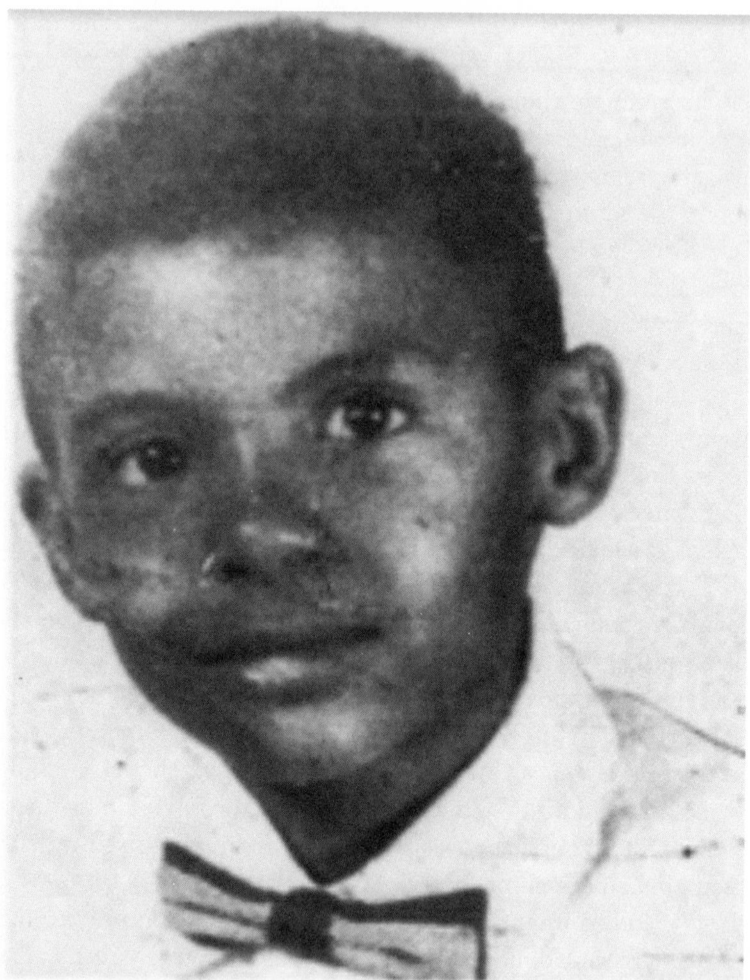

Easter Sunday at age three
COURTESY OF THE AUTHOR

didn't get one. Right then, I learned that there would be big trouble if I didn't obey my elders.

Don't get me wrong, I got my share of spankings. I was a mischievous kid, clumsy, and a slow learner, no matter how hard I tried to be good, while Bobby caught on much faster than I did after just that one spanking from Granny.

But there was never a single moment when we doubted how much she loved us, and we loved her too. She would lay us on the floor and tickle our bellies until we laughed so hard we'd cry. She was mixed-race, a mulatto, with straight hair that hung down to the floor. She liked having me brush her hair and play with it.

Sometimes, while I brushed her hair, she would say in a soft voice, "Granny will be going away soon."

I would ask where she was going, but she would never explain. I was too young to understand what she meant; I just knew I didn't ever want to be apart from her.

Every night she would have Bobby and me kneel beside our bed, put our hands together under our chins, and recite the Lord's Prayer. She always told us, "Honey, anytime you feel that your life is in danger, or you're in trouble, just stop what you're doing and say the Lord's Prayer." I've used that advice my whole life.

We were a religious family, but as the saying goes, "Trust in God, but row for the shore." You can't survive on prayer alone. Prayer didn't put food on the table or clothes on our backs, or heat an ice-cold farmhouse, and living on a farm meant that everyone had a job. Bobby and I had chores every day. We gathered eggs from the chicken coop. We shelled peas into the bath and laundry tub until there were blisters on my four-year-old fingers. We shucked corn into that same tub, and we fed the cows, pigs, and chickens.

If we did all our chores and behaved ourselves, we got to make a trip to the market for Granny, where we'd trade some of our farm produce for things we needed, like kerosene for the lamps in the house, or bags of flour to bake bread.

When Daddy was in a good mood, he'd take us to the market in his white Ford Country Squire station wagon that had real wooden panels on the side. When he didn't take us, Granny's mother, a white woman we called Aunt Sally, would drive us there in her new red Ford pickup truck.

Bobby and I loved going to the market, especially in Daddy's old car. We couldn't wait to burst through those market doors and head straight for the glass counter beside the cash register, where there were buckets of penny candies and rows and rows of candy bars. All that candy in one place looked like some magical illusion that might vanish into thin air at any second.

But not even the sight of all that candy was as exciting as the even bigger deal about those trips to the market: Going there was almost the only time we saw life away from the farm. The country was a great place to grow up, but it was as tough as it was beautiful. The harsh Kansas climate could erode your soul. Whether it was the blistering humid heat of summer, when the wind could suddenly spin out of control into a twister on any given day, or the below-zero iciness of winter that seemed to bring the whole world to a frozen halt, we were always keeping a close eye on the weather and adjusting to it as best we could—in the end, I guess, a fair price to pay for those amber waves of grain.

Our other glimpses of life outside the farm were our rare visits to the rest of our family. One time Daddy drove us to Garnett, Kansas, to see his father, my grandfather Ulysses Tolson, whose brother Melvin was one of the important young men portrayed in the 2007 film *The Great Debaters* with Denzel Washington. Grandpa would tell us stories about his life, and we'd happily sit for hours at a time listening to him, mesmerized.

On my mother's side, my uncle James Madison was a Buffalo Soldier, a name given to African-American US Army regiments. Uncle James had served his country with distinction and loved to share his stories with us as well.

As I listened proudly to my family elders, all they'd accomplished and all they'd sacrificed, I'd fantasize that someday I would do something to carry on their legacy. Something special. Something that mattered. I was still years away from my "Wilt Chamberlain revelation," so I couldn't begin to imagine what that "something" could possibly be, let alone how to get there.

I never doubted that whatever it was, it would involve a lot of hard work, and my parents set great examples when it came to that. They were the polar opposites of laziness when it came to the farm. Neither of them had a high school education, although Mother would eventually get her GED. In spite of that, they were both very bright, honing their down-to-earth common sense with sharp, hard-won survival skills. Unfortunately, that wasn't enough to keep them together.

Daddy was both physically and verbally abusive to Mother. Their loud arguments would turn to physical fights sometimes, and they'd really go at it. Tensions began running higher and higher until they caused a rift between Mother's and Daddy's sides of the family. It got so ugly that my mother's brothers, Uncle Raymond and Uncle Tiken, drove in from Kansas City one day and told my father that if he ever put his hands on their sister again, he'd live to regret it.

And that's when Daddy left us.

All of a sudden, there was no more food, no more wood chopped for the stove, no more rides to the market in his station wagon . . . no way to survive. So early one cold morning in 1956, in drifting, waist-high snow, Uncle Raymond and Uncle Tiken showed up at the farm in a new Oldsmobile 98 and moved Mother, Granny, Bobby, and me to Kansas City, Missouri.

I was only five years old, but I still remember that one-hour car ride—the blur of the snowy white countryside at sunset, and then, suddenly, when night fell, the bright lights of the city. Millions of them. The brightest light I'd ever seen in my life. Next thing I knew, we were on the Plaza, a famous landmark for holiday lights and decorations. I looked around in nothing short of awe and shouted, "Uncle Raymond, Christmas! Christmas, everywhere!"

Kansas City felt like a whole other planet from Bonner Springs. There were streetlights. We had indoor plumbing. Gas stoves, and heat with no need for firewood. Warm beds to sleep in. The United States was just coming out of a recession, and people were poor, but there was work for those who could find it—and tolerate it. Kansas City, Missouri, had two big industries: slaughterhouses for cows, pigs, and chickens; and places where you could eat those cows, pigs, and chickens. Kansas City was known as the Barbecue Capital of the United States, so famous for its barbecue that even US presidents stopped in to eat at Bryant's Bar-B-Q on 18th and Vine. So Mother was able to get a job once we got settled, and she divorced Daddy. Things were way better for my family . . . until they weren't.

Daddy may have left through the front door, but from time to time he managed to reappear through the back. Even though he and Mother were divorced, he kept bouncing in and out of our lives, until there weren't just two of us kids anymore, there were five—and no Daddy again, and no money.

Luckily, Mother was able to look to her brothers for help, two of the hardest-working men I've ever known. Uncle Raymond worked at Lincoln Junior High School, and Uncle Tiken at the Wonder Bread Bakery. They made good money for those days. They lived together in a big, fine house, and they bought a brand new Oldsmobile 98 every year or so. Tiken even became known in the community for how immaculately he maintained his car, so that when it was time for a new one, he had a waiting list of people wanting to buy it.

My uncles were good to us, and filled in for my father in so many ways. Uncle Tiken even gave me my first job and taught me how to earn a dollar, and the value of that dollar. "Son," he said, "if you come to my house every Saturday morning at eight o'clock, I'll pay you two dollars a week to wash the tires on my car." I never missed a Saturday, and he never missed paying me. Then I'd go home and give my three brothers and my sister a quarter each so they could buy penny candy. It made me feel so good to do that for them, and to see how excited it made them.

With Granny's help, Mother raised five kids, all under 12 years old, in a two-bedroom apartment in the Wayne Miner projects, while working three jobs. During the day, from eight in the morning until three in the afternoon, she worked at Menorah Hospital as an assistant nurse. From three until seven, she sewed clothing at a factory. Then she'd come home and do ironing for rich white people from 7:00 to 10:00 at night. I can see her to this day, bone tired, pressing white people's dress shirts and even their sheets. Once in a while she'd fall asleep, standing at the ironing board with the hot iron burning into a sheet, and believe me, that burned sheet smell is something that stays with you for decades.

And then there was school. Kind of. Mother took Bobby, Brent (the first-born after our parents' divorce, the son Daddy claimed wasn't his), and me to D. A. Holmes Elementary School and dropped the younger two, Barry and Boni, at the babysitter's house on her way to her first job.

At that time, Bobby and I thought school was just a place where kids went to play and hang out all day. Other than that, we couldn't be bothered with reading or homework or anything else the teachers seemed to be blathering about.

Granny and Mother's older sister Aunt Helen did most of the babysitting, which wasn't easy, since Mother didn't want any of her children going outside. She was afraid we were likely to get jumped, and she was right. When I went to the grocery store for her and Granny, I would have to hide the money in my shoe in case the older kids chased me and shook me down for whatever I had. Even going to the park by ourselves was off-limits. The last thing she needed was one of us getting in trouble. If she had to leave work because of something we did, it meant an automatic whipping.

She kept up that same grinding, exhausting, merciless schedule every single day, doing everything she possibly could to keep her family together and provide for us. But finally, probably inevitably, it all came crashing down on her, and she had her first nervous breakdown.

What I remember most was her gathering Bobby, Brent, and me at the kitchen table very early one morning and saying, "You kids are just too much for me to handle anymore by myself. Y'all got no dad, and it's killing me. So y'all are going away for a while."

We boys looked at each other. We didn't know what that meant, but we knew it wasn't good when she started crying.

"I can't do this anymore. I've had it up to here." She raised her right hand over her head. She was choking up, and we were staring at her by now—we only saw her like this when something really bad was going on. And sure enough, it was, something worse than we could ever have seen coming. She took a breath and tried to collect herself. Then she dropped the bomb that changed our lives.

"Y'all are going to the orphan home."

I didn't have a clue what an "orphan home" was, but whatever it was, it scared me to death. She told us over and over how sorry she was, and how hard she'd tried to keep this from happening. As she hugged us and cried some more, she added, "You have to leave today. We'll all go to the orphan home together, and then I'll go to work. Do y'all understand?"

Somehow I pieced together that apparently we wouldn't be living at home anymore, and I began to cry as well, which made my brothers cry too.

I finally caught my breath enough to ask, "Mother, when you gonna come back and get us?"

She said she didn't know and started crying even harder. I knew then that we'd be staying there a good while, waiting for her to bring us back home.

"Your little brother and sister are going into foster care. But you three boys are old enough . . . you have to understand, I got no choice. I can't afford . . ."

"We know, Mother," I managed to assure her, while the truth was, I didn't know at all. But the next thing I *did* know, we'd packed what few clothes we had and boarded a metro-city bus with Mother, who left us there at the curb in front of a big brick building called the Niles Home for Orphan Children.

I was nine years old, and I felt abandoned, and lost, and confused, too hopeless to even think about that NBA dream, as if it only existed in a house I didn't live in anymore. I wondered if I'd ever see my sister Boni and my baby brother Barry again. I wondered if I'd ever see Mother, or Granny, or my uncles again. I wondered if I'd ever see anything familiar again in my whole life, or feel safe . . .

My world had just come crashing down, and I was terrified.

Chapter Two

I still remember the frigid walk up that snow-shoveled sidewalk with my little bag of belongings and stepping through the front door of the Niles Home for Orphan Children. Just when I thought the hollow pit in my stomach couldn't get any deeper, my brothers and I were greeted by the sight of Christmas decorations. Everywhere. In all the common areas. It hit me like a cruel joke to remind us that Christmas was right around the corner and we'd be spending it in an orphanage, and

Niles Home, orphanage for children aged nine to fourteen
COURTESY OF THE AUTHOR

I stood there in the entryway for a minute or two taking deep breaths to keep from bursting into tears.

There were also some white people around. It turned out they'd been appointed by the state of Missouri to make sure we children were being properly cared for, and that the facility was being run according to code. I'd never been around a lot of white people, and I kept my distance for a while because I didn't know what to expect from them. But they seemed okay for the most part, and it was reassuring to discover that most of the other kids and workers were Black.

The director of the place was a tight-faced Black man named Mr. Jordan. He was also the chief disciplinarian. His form of discipline was belt-whipping when any of us misbehaved or were slow to obey. With 150 inner-city boys and 150 inner-city girls living there, Mr. Jordan never ran out of opportunities to pull out that belt.

If you got the call to go to Mr. Jordan's office, you knew it wasn't so he could invite you to join him for lunch. I was summoned to that office often enough that I learned how to survive it—I would pad the backside of my jeans with a small towel so the belt wouldn't sting quite so much. Then, during the whipping, I would holler and fake-cry at the top of my lungs, which usually made him stop, at least until next time. Bobby and Brent and I had figured out early on that the only way to survive this place was by sticking together, so I shared that survival technique with them, and it helped, as best it could.

Today Mr. Jordan's style of discipline would land him in jail. But back then it was considered normal, and it made the Niles Home for Orphan Children feel more like a prison than a "home."

I was a nervous kid to begin with, and the whippings I got growing up made me anxious all the time about doing something wrong. I was born with a weak bladder. In fact, I wet the bed until I was 16 years old. My mother and grandmother would give me whippings for it, but instead of getting used to it (both the peeing and the punishment), there were a lot of nights when I'd be too scared to get any sleep at all. The added pressure of living in the orphanage made it worse. Sometimes I would crawl into bed with the other kids in the dormitory and pee on them while they slept to make it look as if it was their fault instead of mine.

We had a housemother named Mrs. Radford who stayed in our dorm with us all night to make sure we didn't run rampant and tear the place up. She would try to wake me up often enough to use the bathroom, but it was usually too late, my bed would already be wet. The only thing that made me feel a little better was that a buddy and dormmate named Cisco Dean wet his bed more often than I wet mine. Sometimes I even had dreams about being in peeing contests with Cisco. It was such a big deal to me that—and this is the truth—I still remember like it was yesterday that hot scald of pee on my skin, and the feel of cold pee that woke me up when I rolled over onto a wet spot on my mattress. It smelled salty, and more than once I caught a whiff of it in my sleep and woke up thinking I was on a beach somewhere.

There were some good kids in the orphanage. There were also some really bad ones. The biggest bully in the place was a guy named Fentress. He had a pair of boxing gloves, and he'd put them on and go walking around just punching people in the face for the fun of it. He thought it was hilarious when he did it to me and busted my nose. He was about 13 years old, and I was nine, so I was easy pickings for him. I don't mind admitting that I was scared of him.

Finally one day my brother Bobby and decided we'd had enough. We double-teamed Fentress and beat the shit out of him. He left us alone after that, but I never could have made it happen without Bobby, which led to one of the most valuable lessons I learned in that orphan home: You always have to be ready to protect *yourself*, because no brother or friend or loved one can be with you 100 percent of the time.

Mrs. Radford liked to save up some cash in a little metal box to pay for some kind of special entertainment for us on Christmas Day. Fentress found out about it, climbed up the side of the building and broke the latch on the window, let himself in, and snuck into Mrs. Radford's room. It took him no time at all to find that metal box in her dresser drawer and steal that Christmas money. Mrs. Radford reported the theft to Mr. Jordan. It didn't take them long to figure out the identity of the thief, and Mr. Jordan called the police and kicked Fentress out of the orphanage. A few weeks later we heard that he broke into some man's house to burglarize it, thinking the house was empty. It wasn't. The owner discovered Fentress, caught him in the act, and shot him dead.

Trouble wasn't hard to find in Kansas City, and even the dumbest, most impulsive idea could cost you your life.

The one saving grace of the Niles Home for Orphan Children was the basketball hoop in the yard. By the time I was 12 years old, I was six feet tall, and I could play way better than any of the other kids. I could even touch the rim of the hoop, while it was all they could do to touch the bottom of the net. No doubt about it, I was a star in that yard.

In school, however, not so much. School was Crispus B. Attucks Elementary, less than a mile from the orphan home. (I'd learned from my uncle that Crispus Attucks was a real man, a slave, and the first American casualty of the Revolutionary War. He was of African and American Indian descent, just like me—my daddy's ancestors were Kansas Blackfoot Indians.) We'd all walk to school in clothes from the orphanage: white T-shirts, blue jeans, and tennis shoes. If your shoes got worn out from running around in them, too bad, you had to wear them anyway. I was one of the tallest kids in school, almost as tall as my teachers, so my clothes hardly ever fit, even when they were new. My pants were what we called "highwaters," with the cuffs about two or three inches above my shoes. Kids would constantly make fun of me because of my clothes, in that cruel, brutally honest way kids love to tease.

School always felt to me like as bad a fit as my clothes. It was an inner-city public school, where misbehaving was a lot more important than studying, and the only way I could hope to excel was to try to be the most hilarious class clown in Attucks Elementary history.

Somehow, I didn't have my first taste of real academic failure until fifth grade. I flunked the first time around, and I was well on my way to flunking again. It shouldn't have been a surprise—I couldn't read or write, and math was a complete mystery. All through school up to that point, school had meant nothing but playtime to me. I wasn't learning a thing, so I'd just act out instead to kill time. But fifth grade is when classwork starts to get more serious, and when you're illiterate, you have no idea what's going on, which leads to nothing but nonstop frustration. Back then, there was no one to sit down with me and figure out if maybe I had a learning disability, or if working with a tutor could help me get on track. It was just sink or swim, and I was sinking.

School had never been a priority at home. Daddy wasn't around, and Mother's education ended with the eighth grade. The only reading material in our house were issues of *Ebony* and *Jet* and the *Kansas City Star*. That was it. There were no books, and there was no one to read to me at bedtime with Mother being so busy working. The only time she was involved in what was happening at school was when there was a problem serious enough for her to get a call from a teacher or the principal and she had to show up in person. Then it became *our* problem, usually punctuated by a whipping when we got home.

The fifth grade teacher who was about to flunk me for the second time was a woman named Mrs. Captoria Fox. To me she was a mean-eyed, hard-hearted old woman. She also happened to be a cousin on my father's side of the family. When Mother heard that I was about to be held back again, she marched to the school, squared off with Mrs. Fox, and stuck up for me.

Mother was a lovely breeze of a person, even when she was angry, but if she thought one of her kids was being treated unfairly, she never backed down. When it became obvious that she and Mrs. Fox were never going to see eye to eye, she went straight to the principal's office to plead my case.

"My son Dean is already the tallest kid in his class," she pointed out. "Imagine how hard that's going to be on him if he's held back for two years in a row."

She begged him to pass me on to sixth grade, and he did. The subject of my being illiterate never came up. And the fact that, thanks to Mother, the school principal overrode Mrs. Fox's decision caused even more fallout between Mother's and Daddy's sides of the family.

I had no way of knowing it at the time, but being promoted without being able to read or write would become a pattern throughout my school years. The better I got at basketball as a teenager, the more automatically I was passed on from one grade to the next without ever understanding any of the classes, right on through my senior year at the University of Arkansas at the age of 21.

When I wasn't in school, I was at the orphanage, just trying to survive with my brothers and avoid beatings as best we could. On many nights I would lie awake in the dark, when no one could see me cry, wondering if Mother would ever take us home. Between her long shifts at the hospital and the fact that the orphan home administrators only wanted parents to visit on weekends, she only came to see us for an hour or so every few weeks. I'd get my hopes up every time, thinking maybe she'd finally say, "Pack your things and come with me," but it kept not happening.

A lot of parents never came back, leaving the kids to live on meaningless words and broken promises, and that scared us half to death. If it could happen to them, it could happen to us. All we ever thought about was getting out of that place, but we had no say in that, no way to control it or behave our way out of there, and it was the most powerless, empty feeling I could ever imagine.

And then one day in July of 1963, the summer before Bobby was about to start high school and age out of the system, Mother came to pick us up and take us home. She told us later that there was no way she would have taken Bobby and left Brent and me at the orphanage. I was so grateful I was literally speechless, which had never happened to me before (or maybe since).

It had been five years. Five years that seemed like an eternity, five years in what was essentially an emotional prison. Walking out of there with my mother and brothers felt like the weight of the world had been lifted off my shoulders and my soul, and it was the most exhilarating day of my life.

As an added, unbelievable bonus, not only were we going home, we were going home to *our own house*, where Boni and Barry and Granny were waiting to welcome us with open arms.

It was a long-awaited dream come true, a dream I'd been too afraid to even let myself think about—we were a family again.

I'd be going to a new school.

My NBA fantasy would become my obsession.

The orphanage was in my rear view mirror forever, and I was the happiest kid on earth.

Chapter Three

As soon as we'd settled in, Bobby, Brent, and I were dying to hear where this new house came from. Mother had always been light years away from being able to buy a house, no matter how hard she worked. But it seems that in 1962, the year before we'd been sprung from the orphanage, Granny started receiving her monthly Social Security checks, and by pooling those checks and Mother's salary, the two of them were able to come up with the down payment, pay the $75-a-month mortgage, and still manage to take care of five children. So it was goodbye Wayne Miner projects, and hello 3315 Olive Street.

Whether or not it was a coincidence we'll never know, but around that time, Daddy suddenly appeared at the Olive Street house. Of course, he'd never offered a single dime of support for Mother or any of us kids, and the last thing she needed was another mouth to feed, so she didn't exactly give him a warm welcome.

Neither did Granny. When he showed up again, she planted herself at the front door. I was standing right behind her, and the image is still locked in my mind—my strong, fierce granny, hair tied back in a bun, and her right hand gripping the claw hammer she'd grabbed when she realized who'd come knocking.

"Stand back, boy!" she commanded me, and then shouted at Daddy through the closed door, "You're not welcome here! This house belongs to me and my daughter! Stay away from us or I will lay this hammer upside your head, Nigga! I mean it!"

Daddy had been around Granny too long to test her. He left. Permanently.

So then it was just us—Mother, Granny, five young children, and our Aunt Helen, who was struggling with a mental illness and couldn't live on her own anymore.

We also had a few tenants upstairs over the years. The one I remember most was a man named Joe Nunley. Mr. Nunley was a World War II veteran who was "shell-shocked" from his years in the armed forces and would often warn us that "the Nazis are coming."

In addition to her other jobs, Mother was sort of a caretaker for Mr. Nunley and earned a little extra money ironing his clothes and helping him with his meals. He would do crazy things sometimes. One night after dinner, we kids scraped leftover food into the garbage as usual. Mr. Nunley reached in, took that food out of the garbage, and ate it. Mother tried to stop him, but he wouldn't let her take his plate away from him.

When I was 13, Mr. Nunley took me to the local car wash where he used to work. He lied and told the boss that I was 16 years old, which was believable thanks to my height, and just like that, I had my first real job. I made $45 a week and gave Mother $20 of it to help with the bills.

Mother was working nonstop. Granny was getting older, she had diabetes, and she had her hands full taking care of Aunt Helen. Bobby had become rebellious since we got home from the orphanage and wasn't around very much. So in addition to earning money to help the family, I was also starting to watch over the younger kids more than ever.

Mother still never wanted us venturing too far from home and getting into the trouble that was lurking around every corner, which made it necessary for me to come up with activities to keep my siblings occupied. One of our favorites was watching cartoons together on our little black-and-white television and then drawing the characters we'd just seen on TV. My sister Boni, the youngest, really struggled with drawing, but she kept at it, and it paid off—she grew up to be an artist and taught art to kids.

Mother had me take my brothers and sister to the store every day, where we'd buy a half gallon of milk, which was all the milk we could afford. A half gallon of milk happened to equal five cups, so each of us kids were allowed one cup per day. We could do anything we wanted with it—drink it, pour it on our cereal, even pour it on our heads if we wanted.

But it was a strict one-cup limit, and if we took someone else's, or tried to sneak a little extra for ourselves, we'd get a whipping.

It was all part of growing up poor, but rather than focusing on what we didn't have, we were happy knowing that we finally had each other again after being separated for five years. There was joy in getting reacquainted and finding our way back, together, to our family's definition of "normal."

Sometimes we'd sneak into other people's yards and pick apples from their trees. We didn't think it was wrong. They had more apples than they could ever eat, and to us it was another group adventure, with the excuse that we were helping provide fresh fruit for our pantry.

Then there was our first Christmas in our new house. I wanted it to be special, so I crept into a neighbor's yard, cut down one of their trees, and dragged it home to make sure we had a Christmas tree. Not to be outdone, Boni and Barry snuck across the street and "borrowed" some lightbulbs from their decorations to replace our burned-out and broken ones.

Mischievous? Absolutely. Shouldn't have? No doubt about it. But we never did any of those things with malice or bad intentions; we were just trying so hard to live like a real family who could afford all the fresh food and Christmas decorations they wanted.

The people across the street from us at 3306 Olive Street, the ones with the depleted Christmas lights, were the Stricklands. They were the model Black family in the neighborhood, with a new car, a nice house, and money. The mother was Jothana, and the father was Robert Sr., and there were five children in the family, just like us: Bobby, Donnie, Cheryl, Michele, and Teresa.

And just like me, the boys, Bobby and Donnie, who were both older than I was, dreamed of playing professional sports. They had a basketball hoop in their backyard, and when I wasn't shooting hoops in school, I was playing at the Stricklands'.

Bobby and Donnie played baseball, football, and basketball in a church league, and it was thanks to them that I got to play organized basketball for the first time. All the kids on both teams had uniforms with numbers on the back of their jerseys. There were two coaches, and two referees, the closest I'd ever come to real basketball, and I loved it! After the games, Mr. Strickland always took us to McDonald's and other great places for treats. I couldn't wait to be rich enough to do that for my family someday.

While basketball was becoming a bigger and bigger part of my life, I was struggling worse and worse in school. A brand new schoolhouse had just been built only two blocks from home, so I attended sixth grade at Katherine B. Richardson Elementary, a year behind and *way* taller than my classmates, not to mention skinny and lanky.

Of course, that set me up as a target for relentless bullying by other boys at school and in my neighborhood. Before long, though, they found out that I could punch knots on their heads faster than they could come up with another nasty name to call me. I'd learned to fight in the orphanage, where it was all about survival. In the "real" world, especially at school, fighting turned out to be all about getting me in a whole lot of trouble.

When Mother had finally exhausted every other option she could think of to keep me from fighting, she saw to it that I started the seventh grade at Lincoln Junior High. The reason: My Uncle Raymond worked there as a janitor. He was a good man, the father figure I'd never had, and the guy who kept me out of (most) fights.

Uncle Raymond also did something for me that no one else could possibly have done—he let me into the gymnasium after school every afternoon, and I'd practice basketball while he mopped, waxed, and buffed the floors in that brand new building. I still remember the first time I stepped into that gym and saw the polished hardwood court, with two big beautiful glass backboards and clean, perfectly tied nets on the hoops at either end. It was basketball heaven, and when I was in that magical place, nothing else mattered, or even existed.

From that first moment on, I'd spend the whole day doing nothing but wait for the final bell to ring. Then I'd race out to sit by the schoolyard flagpole, where Uncle Raymond would meet me, walk me to the gym door, unlock it for me, and go on about his business. I would stay for hours, working hard on jump shots, turnaround jumpers, bank shots, half-court shots, every move in the game. Finally, at dusk, in the diminishing light that seeped through the windows, my workout would end when I'd hear Uncle Raymond, finished cleaning for the day, yell, "Closing time!" and we'd catch the bus together in the dark and head home.

Other than that, I hated every minute of being in that building, wedging my big body into those tiny desks, hour after hour, unable to read or write or understand anything the teacher was droning on about, cutting up, trying to find any way I could to make time go faster while I waited to meet up with Uncle Raymond at the flagpole, relieved that another day of agony was over with.

Eventually, maybe inevitably, I started skipping classes, heading to the playground and just hanging out, listening for that final bell. Unbeknownst to me until it was too late, our principal, Dr. Campbell, routinely walked the school grounds looking for kids who were cutting class. And sure enough, he caught me.

My punishment, he told me, was going to be 10 swats on my behind with a paddle. He had a problem, though—I was 6'1", and he was maybe 5'11" with his shoes on. I'd been getting whipped my whole life, by Mother, by Granny, by Mr. Jordan at the orphan home . . . I was done. No more.

I looked down at him and laid it out: "I'll take one swat a day, and that's it."

At that moment, Uncle Raymond suddenly appeared. He'd heard the whole thing, and he pulled me aside, out of Dr. Campbell's earshot.

"Son," he said, "you need to take those swats. If you don't, they're not gonna pass you, and you'll be coming back here for eighth grade again. Is that what you want?"

Obviously, it wasn't. All I wanted, all I was looking forward to in my whole life, was to move on, play basketball in high school, and get another step closer to the NBA.

I walked back to Dr. Campbell and took the 10 swats.

I also swore it was the last time a principal would put his hands on me. Ever.

Chapter Four

I'm sure it was partly due to following Uncle Raymond's advice and taking those 10 swats from Dr. Campbell that I made it through eighth grade at Lincoln Junior High and headed on to Central Senior High at 33rd and Indiana. They were basketball champions. Local heroes. The kids at Lincoln called me a traitor because I became a Central High Blue Eagle instead of a Lincoln High Tiger.

In the meantime, Mother had started working the evening shift as a waitress at a bar on Prospect Avenue. That's where she met my soon-to-be stepfather, Eddie Jones. Eddie was a construction worker who made decent money, and he was one of the bar regulars.

Not long after Mother married Eddie, Granny passed away. It was the first time I'd experienced the death of someone I loved, and it crushed me. I remember standing beside her open casket at the viewing, trying to process what was happening. I kept staring at her face, silently willing her to open her eyes and come back home with us where she belonged, because she was Granny and she couldn't possibly be gone, until I heard Eddie say, "I think somebody better go get Dean," and someone put their arm around my shoulder and led me away.

Eddie seemed to be a good guy at first, and not long after he moved into the house, he went out and got a wooden backboard and a hoop and put it up over the garage. He also got me one of those old orange Voit rubber basketballs, the kind you get when you can't afford the nicer Spalding or Wilson balls. I finally had a ball of my own and a place to work out with it, so I could shoot baskets and stay out of the parks like Mother asked.

So there I was in the driveway one day, dazzling a huge imaginary crowd with my dunking skills, when I jumped for a rebound, touched the backboard, and landed with a giant wood splinter in my hand. I was in excruciating pain for weeks. My teachers kept sending notes home to Mother saying, "Please take Dean to the doctor," and she did. But every time we went, they claimed they couldn't find anything.

Mother made me soak my hand, then soak it again, and then soak it some more. Nothing. Finally, one night when the pain was keeping me awake, Eddie got out of bed, sat down beside me, took my hand, and starting rubbing it hard. It hurt like hell, but all of a sudden that splinter popped out of my hand, landed right on my face, and stuck to it because of the pus. I still consider myself lucky that I didn't get gangrene from it—it would have ended my basketball career before it even got started.

Mother told me many years later that she married Eddie because he promised to help her take care of us. It didn't take her long to figure out that Eddie's definition of "help" had nothing to do with money. He never paid a single bill, and two years later he was out of there and we were on our own again. After he left, we moved to a house at 45th and Prospect, down the street from where she was working. And somehow, through all that, my focus never wavered, not once.

Basketball was becoming a bigger and bigger part of my life. The Central High Blue Eagles had been winning the Missouri State Men's Basketball Championship every year under Coach Jim Wilkerson, and I wanted more than anything else in this world to be part of it and play for that talented man. However, in order to make that wish come true and elevate my status with the team, I had to go through an initiation process.

Here's how that went:

I got jumped on by gang members almost every other day, to prove I was tough enough to take the punishment and fight back. It wasn't unusual for those gang members to terrorize their targets right out of school, especially since they were known to always have their guns with them.

There were four possible responses to these gangsters. You could be a fool and show them you were scared to death; you could drop off the basketball team; you could act like a punk and transfer to another high school where you didn't have to fight every day; or you could fight them back.

I chose to fight them back. I even had my mother's permission. Central had such a reputation for fighting that the schools at the Interscholastic League Field House where we played only scheduled daytime games, to avoid the Blue Eagles playing there at night.

One day I was standing in line, waiting to buy my hot school lunch with the 35 cents Mother had given me, when a kid named James Wilcox stepped up to me. I didn't know him, or anything about him, but I found out later that he was nobody to mess with. He was a gang leader. He dressed like a gangster, he walked like a gangster, he carried a gun like a gangster, and according to his reputation, he'd killed two people, execution style, by the time he turned 18.

But when he got in my face and demanded I give him a "protection fee," I didn't reach for my wallet, I just asked, "What for?"

He had a smile like a snake. "To keep my boys from jumping on you every day after school. Your safety is in real jeopardy if you don't pay, Nigga. Understand?"

"How much is your protection fee?"

"Your lunch money. Thirty-five cents. From now on."

Well, that choice was simple enough. Apparently, the only way I'd get my lunch every day was if I kept my 35 cents, ate a hot meal, and waited for the fight after school.

So I was right back in the fighting game. James and 10 of his hoodlums chased me and some other kids that day. But I could run faster than hellfire, and after about 10 blocks, James was the only one who was still coming after me.

I stopped running, politely walked back to him, and offered to kick his ass. I couldn't whip 10, I told him, even when those 10 were cowards and definitely not distance runners. I could whip one, though, and if this was all about seeing if I was scared, sorry to disappoint him, but I wasn't. And with that, I kicked his ass, and from then on, they were out to kill me.

Somewhere deep inside me, I knew that all this confrontation stuff was some kind of preparation. If I was to play basketball on any kind of competitive or professional level, I couldn't afford to be scared of *anybody*.

I went out for basketball my freshman year, but I got cut from the team before a game by Coach Williams, the freshman coach, who was a cousin on my mother's side of the family. It had nothing to do with my not being good enough; it had to do with what had happened at home earlier that morning. Mother had asked me to help her with some chores before I left the house to catch the team bus. I was worried about being late for that bus, but she couldn't have cared less about basketball; she only cared that I listened to her, which I did.

I finished the chores, ran out the door, and raced through an obstacle course of rain puddles and mud piles to catch the team bus. By the time I got there, I was a filthy mess.

Coach Williams took one look at me and sneered, "You're an embarrassment, and a disgrace to the team. You're not getting on this bus. Go home and come back next year when you get your shoes cleaned off, Buster."

I couldn't believe my ears. "Coach, it's not going to take me a whole year to clean this mud off my shoes."

"Tough luck," he replied as he turned his back, disappeared back into the bus, and it pulled off without me.

I was down, but I wasn't out. If I couldn't play basketball on the freshman team, I'd just try some other sport. I went out for track and made the team running the 440 relay and doing the long jump and high jump. I also ran a few cross-country races and took win, place, or show in all of them.

And what do you know, it was because of track, not basketball, that Coach Wilkerson, Central's varsity coach, spotted my athletic ability and invited me to try out for his team.

I'd never quit working on my basketball game. I played pickup ball every chance I got at the Boys Club, the YMCA, community centers, college gymnasiums, anywhere and everywhere I could find. For added motivation, the Strickland brothers had made the varsity basketball team,

Bobby as a senior and Donnie as a junior. Their photos kept showing up in the *Kansas City Star* after Friday and Saturday varsity games, and I wanted *my* photo in there too.

So yes, thank you, Coach Wilkerson, I'd love to try out for your team. I did, and I made it, not only the junior varsity team in 1968 but also the varsity team, suiting up for both games. I rarely got to play my sophomore year, but in my junior and senior years I played the whole game every game. I made first-team All-State my senior year and became the top player in the whole state of Missouri. In fact, the coach ended up cutting Bobby Strickland, and I took his place. I really felt bad about that, since Bobby was one of the first guys who taught me how to actually play the game. But at age 16, I was 6-feet-4-inches tall, and that helped a lot. I was building a reputation as one hell of a player and a guy to watch in Kansas City. Suddenly, it seemed as if everyone had heard of this kid named Dean Tolson.

Central High had some amazing alumni, one of whom was Warren Jabali Armstrong, who was drafted by the Oakland Oaks in the American Basketball Association (ABA) professional basketball league and was named Rookie of the Year. He came out of Wichita State University and played for the legendary college coach Ralph Miller. Jabali knew the game inside and out, and he was one of my heroes.

As luck would have it, Jabali lived five houses down the street from Uncle Raymond. I'll never forget the first time I met him. I'd just left Uncle Raymond's house, and I was walking home when Jabali pulled up in this brand new, sparkling clean chocolate-brown Mercedes-Benz. I was too busy staring at that car to notice who was driving it, until he yelled, "You play ball, young fella?"

I looked up, instantly recognized him, went into shock, looked down again, and simply nodded, too shy to even raise my head.

"Look at me when I talk to you," he ordered, not unfriendly, just firm.

He hopped out of his car and opened the trunk. It was full of boxes and boxes of basketball sneakers, and I was gaping at them when he said, "They give me a new pair for every game, but I don't always wear them. Take a few pairs for yourself."

I'd admired this guy since the first time I saw him play. He was as tough as they came on the court, and he played with a real attitude and swagger. Suddenly I admired him as much off the court as on—this superstar, this hero, giving away brand new shoes to some tall skinny kid he'd just seen walking down the street. Now I was in awe.

We talked for a few minutes, and from that day on, whenever he came to town to visit, he would pick me up at Uncle Raymond's house in his brand new Mercedes-Benz and say, "Let's go kick some ass." We always did, and I cherished every minute of it. Jabali had 10 brothers and sisters, and he treated me like one of his brothers. Playing with him taught me how to be serious about my game and "better my best."

Thank you, Jabali, from the bottom of my heart, for the rest of my life.

Then, without warning, my focus on basketball was rudely interrupted by what felt like a massive, vicious midwestern tornado. Times were changing around the country, and Kansas City was one of the cores of the madness. Riots broke out in 1968, the Black Panthers invaded Central High School, and I was there.

The Panthers targeted Central High because of its reputation for shootings, murders, stabbings, and gang violence, not to mention more headline-grabbing athletic championships in all sports than any other high school in the city. And then there was the fact that we had 4,000 Black students and no white students. The Black Panthers didn't stop with us, either. They also invaded three other inner-city, all-Black high schools—Manual, Lincoln, and Paseo.

I asked around about the Black Panther Party and found out that when they started the organization, they weren't a Black supremacy, radical, arms-bearing group. Instead, their goal was to maintain a balance between protecting their people and enforcing constitutional rights. But when they came blasting into Central High on April 4, 1968, they came armed to take violent, retributive action against white supremacy.

I was standing in the principal's office, where I was a frequent visitor, when one of the Black Panthers charged in, grabbed the principal by the neck, and shoved the school's intercom microphone up to his mouth. The principal sat there frozen in shocked silence as the Panther barked, "I want you to announce to the students that Martin Luther King has just been assassinated."

I couldn't believe what I was seeing, or what I'd just heard, but I wasn't about to make a sound, thinking that maybe if I didn't draw any attention to myself I could somehow magically disappear.

The principal, as stunned as I was, managed to find his voice for, "Is that all you want me to say?"

"Tell them school is out."

"Starting when?"

"Starting right now!"

The principal hesitated for a moment too long, prompting the Panther, in a low growl, to add what sounded like a promise. "If you don't do it now, you're a dead man."

The principal complied. His hand was shaking when he took the microphone and made the tragic announcement about Dr. King and let school out immediately.

As the kids spilled out of their classrooms, all hell broke loose. The students threw teachers out of windows. They broke the glass trophy cases in the hallways. They poured out into the streets and started setting all the trash cans on fire. Fighting. Looting. Deafening insanity all over the place. It was total chaos. Madness.

Impossible as it seemed, the riots escalated from there. The Black Panthers marshaled 100,000 Black men to go out and burn down the city, chanting, "Burn, baby, burn!" Thousands of kids from Central High formed a kind of tidal wave, crashing toward downtown Kansas City. I was being pushed along with them but not part of them, even though they kept threatening me with a nonstop, "We're going to kick your ass if you don't do what we say."

Before long, students from all four Black schools had assembled and started a peaceful march toward City Hall. But in the pressure-cooker atmosphere of smoke-filled air, ear-shattering noise, and violence, they quickly became violent as well, morphing the march into an out-of-control mob. Police were everywhere, spraying mace and tear gas. The looting and property damage spread like cancer. Blocks of houses were set on fire. The governor of Missouri imposed a curfew of six o'clock that night and for the next two weeks, and the police and National Guard were given orders to shoot anyone caught on the streets after curfew.

At the first sight of the National Guard, I split off from the horror around me and hurried home. But the rioting continued for hours . . . days . . . weeks.

Meanwhile, unbelievably, something incredible was happening in my life. I'd been contacted by Coach Lanny Van Eman of the University of Arkansas, saying he wanted to recruit me. So a few days after the war zone riots started, not having realized the severity of the siege Kansas City was under or the danger he could be in just by being there, Van Eman was actually sitting in our living room to sell me and Mother on the idea of my enrolling at the university and playing basketball for the Arkansas Razorbacks. He was explaining the recruiting process when we heard a loud rumbling noise outside that seemed to be headed straight for us.

Coach Van Eman stopped in mid-sentence and asked, "What in the hell is that noise out there that's shaking the house?"

Mother, very concerned, replied, "Heck if I know."

My brothers and sister had joined us in the living room, and we all ran to the window to see two huge National Guard tanks rolling up the street, carrying soldiers with .50-caliber machine guns poised and ready. Seconds later, the soldiers opened fire on a vehicle in the street across from our house.

The people in the car were our neighbors, the Delaneys. A nice, quiet couple. They obviously hadn't heard about the 6:00 p.m. curfew, or hoped they could evade it long enough for Mr. Delaney to drive his wife to work. Fortunately—actually, miraculously—the Delaneys didn't get hit, even though their car was pretty much destroyed, and we never saw them again.

The city-wide curfew lasted two weeks before peace was restored. Six people were killed in those two weeks, and $4 million worth of damage was done. The 1968 riots were triggered by a specific, unspeakable tragedy and the assassination of a great man. But they were also the result of long-entrenched tensions throughout the city and the country, of monumental importance in the history of Kansas City, Missouri, and in our nation as well.

As crazy as life was all around us, it was almost as crazy inside our house.

After Daddy left for good, he met and married an 18-year-old white woman named Glenda. They lived across town, and Daddy ended up having five children with her, exactly as he'd done with Mother. True to form, he didn't take care of those kids either.

Some of us would go visit them from time to time. We were lucky enough not to be there the day he got so mad at Glenda that he broke their bed and threw it down the stairs. Once he got all the bed parts and mattresses into the yard, he set them on fire. Then he went back in the house and put his wife and their five kids out on the street.

Mother was horrified when she heard about it, and, knowing Daddy as well as she did, empathetic to her core.

"We can't have them out on the street," she said.

And with that, she brought them all into our house. Including Glenda, who was maybe 22 or 23 years old by then, not all that much older than I was.

I didn't blame Mother one bit, but it made for a way-too-crowded, even more chaotic household. Now that Glenda was around to help watch over everyone and ease a little of the pressure on my mother, I decided it was time for me to get out of there.

Thanks to my last two years of high school, I even had a place to go that would move me one step closer to making my NBA dream come true.

Chapter Five

Lanny Van Eman, head coach of the Arkansas Razorbacks basketball team, had first approached me when I was a sophomore going into my junior year. When I grew four inches, from 6-feet-4 to 6-feet-8 that summer, he became even more interested in me.

By my junior year, Coach Wilkerson had retired and was replaced by Jack Bush, who came from our crosstown rival, Manual High School. My grade point average was under 2.0, but I was leading the team with 20 points and 13 rebounds per game. So Coach Bush kept asking my teachers to give me a passing grade every semester to keep me eligible to play, and they kept obliging. It never mattered to the school, or me, that I still couldn't read or write. As long as I could put a basketball through a hoop and win games, I was welcome at Central High. And at 16 years old, when the Central High Blue Eagles played at the Interscholastic League Field House, with 5,000 people cheering like crazy and my name at the top of the scoring and rebounding lists above the score clock, I couldn't have cared less about my grade point average, or much of anything else.

My junior year on the basketball court was my best yet. I made second-team All-State, and I immediately started getting letters from major colleges around the country. It was common knowledge in the collegiate community that Kansas City, and especially Central High School, was loaded with talented Black athletes, from Omar Hasley, to brothers Raudell and Mervill McMurry, to Ernest Jennings, Melvin Porter, and many others, so scouts from Kansas, Missouri, Oklahoma, and Iowa, just for starters, were inviting me to come visit their campuses.

I went on several of those visits, eager to prove that I could help them win games. Every tryout went great. And every tryout would be followed by a request to see my transcript. As soon as they saw my grades, they'd say, "We'll be in touch," and I would never hear from them again.

So there I was, going into my senior year of high school, and I couldn't even read the recruiting letters that were showing up on a pretty regular basis. I could get by when it came to looking at statistics, and I could more or less understand a newspaper. When I memorized sentences, I could recognize them, or at least parts of them, when I saw them. But if someone handed me a book and told me to read a page, I was out of luck.

Which made it even more ironic that when I was 16, I got a job . . . at the *Kansas City Star.* I started out as a stuffer, tucking the comic strips behind the newspapers' front pages as they rolled off the press. By the end of every night, I had fresh black ink all over my hands and face, and I looked like I'd been in a fight. For all that up-close-and-personal work with words, and earning good money at $10 an hour, I had no idea what any of it said. When I turned 18, I was promoted to copyboy, running copy from the teletype machines to the editors, but I didn't have to read a word there either, I just ran and stayed in shape.

Most people didn't even know that I was illiterate. I could speak well, so people assumed I could read. My white co-workers at the *Kansas City Star* read the newspaper during breaks. Obviously, I didn't, and it was fine with me. As far as I was concerned, the name of the game, for me and for every other Black kid like me, boiled down to one word I *could* read: survival. And for me, survival meant nothing more and nothing less than dominating on the basketball court.

My seriously low grade point average didn't stop several junior colleges from trying to recruit me—they were more than happy to welcome a kid with failing grades if he could help them win. Some guys would go the junior college route and then transfer to a Division I school if they managed to improve their grades. No, thanks. To me, that was a step further away from a future in the NBA, and no way was I going to let that happen.

In the meantime, not a day went by when I wasn't working on my game. Every afternoon, the elite players in Kansas City played pickup basketball at The Boys Club of America at 43rd and Cleveland, and I was there every chance I got.

One day a tall, dark, good-looking man walked in with Lester Burke, the Boys & Girls Club director, during a game. As they passed by, I asked one of my teammates who the stranger was.

"That's Lester Burke's friend Bob Hopkins," he said. "He's a college basketball coach."

The two men took a seat in the bleachers and watched us play. When we finished, Coach Hopkins said to Lester, "I want that kid to go to New Orleans and play for me at Xavier University." He was talking about me!

A week later I was on a plane to New Orleans. Coach Hopkins even knew I was illiterate and told me that if I came to play there, the nuns at Xavier would teach me how to read and write. It sounded like a dream come true.

As if he wasn't already cool enough, he also turned out to be a first cousin of Bill Russell, the legendary NBA Hall of Famer I'd seen on TV when I was nine years old.

I had no idea that Coach Bob Hopkins would end up becoming the reason I eventually got to play in the NBA.

While I was in New Orleans, I met and scrimmaged with a star player at Xavier University who would come to be known as Slick Watts. Great player, great guy, and we'd meet again years later. But at those scrimmages in the Xavier gymnasium, I was all over the court, outplaying everyone and dunking on anyone near me with my 48-inch vertical leap. At one point Slick said, "Man, you jump so high you give me a nosebleed."

After that scrimmage, Coach Hopkins asked me to sign a letter of intent to attend Xavier when I finished my senior year at Central, and that's exactly what I did.

I went back to Kansas City very excited about my future in New Orleans. There were Black people there, and I really liked Coach Hopkins.

Unfortunately, Mother didn't share my excitement. At all. She wanted me to go to the University of Arkansas, and she *really* didn't want me to go to Xavier. To her, Louisiana, and specifically New Orleans, was the home of voodoo, and there was no telling what bad things could happen to me there. And because Xavier was farther away than Arkansas, if something bad *did* happen to me, she wouldn't be able to afford traveling to New Orleans to help me.

I loved her with all my heart, and I cared what she thought. But literally all I could think about was finishing my senior year, moving out of my mother's house and becoming my own man, and heading straight to Xavier to play for Coach Hopkins.

Grades were the last thing on my mind. My teachers and coaches were worried that I wouldn't graduate. I was apparently the only person who *wasn't* worried that I wouldn't graduate. My coaches always took care of that for me, and I knew they wouldn't let me flunk out. Sure, my GPA had fallen to a 1.80 overall, and even the junior colleges who wanted to recruit me were concerned about how low my grades were. But in the end, let's face it, I told myself, they weren't looking for me to shine in class. They wanted to win games, and I was one of their best chances at making that happen.

So rather than worrying about improving my GPA, I focused on having a good year on the court. The Blue Eagles opened the season with a doubleheader in St. Louis, Missouri, against Beaumont and Sumner High Schools. The first night, we beat Beaumont, and I scored 25 points, hitting the winning basket at the buzzer. Walter Williams, an All-American, was supposedly the top player in the state. But after that game, everyone knew the name Dean Tolson.

We were celebrating our victory on the school bus when Beaumont students started throwing bricks at us. One of the bricks crashed through the window and hit a cheerleader in the head. A few shards of glass flew into her eye, and she ended up in the emergency room.

The next night, we had a police escort to the Sumner game. I scored 33 points in that game, but we still lost. Sumner had the tallest high school team I'd ever seen, with David Brent at 7-foot-1 playing center and Harry Rogers at 6-foot-8 playing point guard. They went on to win the men's Missouri State Basketball Championship in the 1969–1970 season.

Before we got off the bus back in Kansas City, Coach Bush gave us a brief, perfect talk that made us all feel better. "Now that we've survived the Land of the Giants with a split," he said, "we can get back to playing

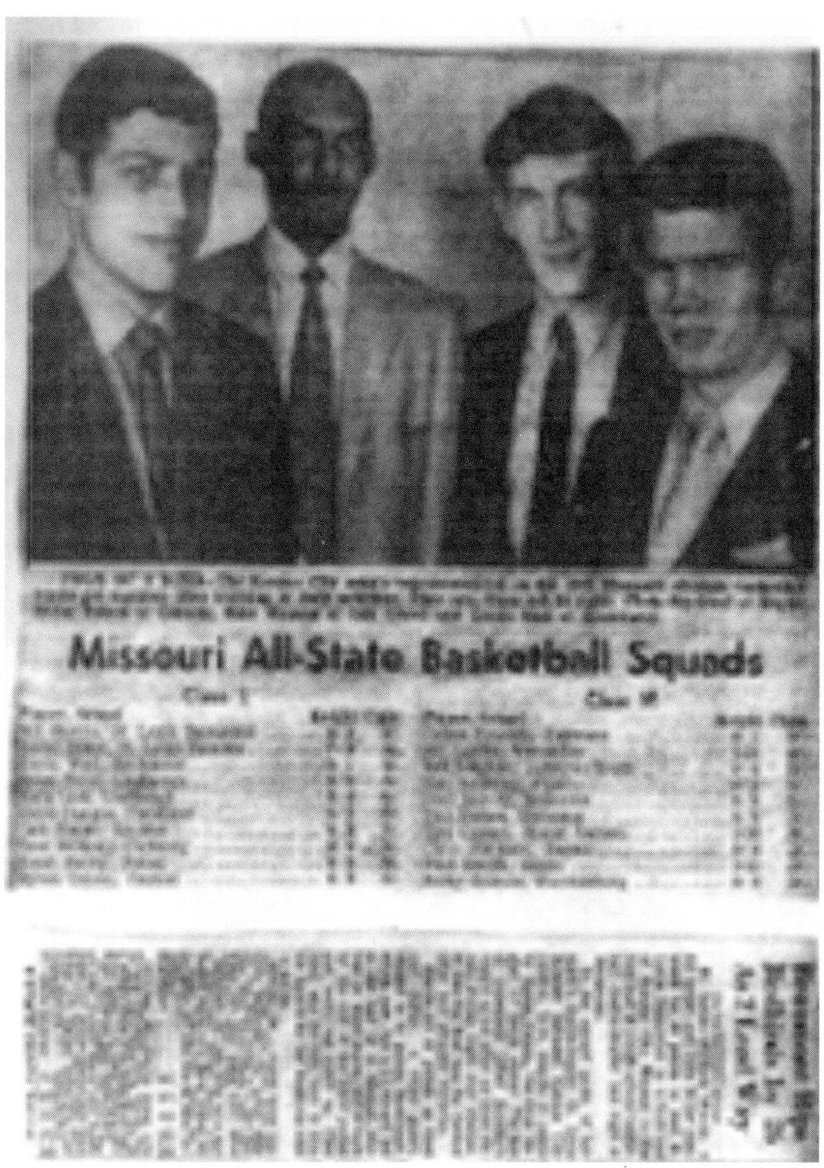

Missouri All-State Basketball Squads

Missouri All-State squad

COURTESY OF THE AUTHOR

normal basketball. We were lucky to win one of those games in St. Louis against Beaumont, and we beat Sumner on the road, so I'd say we have a pretty good team."

I learned a lot about grace from that man.

I got home that night to find a notice in my mailbox, which Mother read to me:

To: Byron Dean Tolson

Military profile photo
COURTESY OF THE AUTHOR

Chapter Five

Greetings. You are hereby ordered for induction into the Armed Forces of the United States of America.

I didn't give it much thought at first. All I had to do was go to the Federal Building in downtown Kansas City and sign in for the draft. I couldn't imagine the government drafting me. I arrived to join a long line of young men, white and Black, standing there, nervous and impatient. It wasn't until then that it hit me what might happen. Then I got scared.

The Vietnam War was raging, and lots of GIs I knew personally were dying over in Southeast Asia. I thought about my recently deceased uncle and honored war hero, Captain Riley Leroy Pitts. His wife, my father's baby sister Eula May Tolson, and their two kids, Stacy and Mark, were honored by President Lyndon Baines Johnson, who presented them with a Purple Heart, a Silver Star, and a Congressional Medal of Honor on behalf of Uncle Riley. My family was very proud of its self-sacrificing heroes.

But I wasn't ready to sacrifice my life on the other side of the world. I stood there in that line thinking, "I don't want to die. I want to play in the NBA. That's my destiny, not being a soldier dying in some godforsaken jungle." Then I noticed a white, square-shouldered man in a military uniform scanning the young men in line, and I went over to try to point out what I thought should have been obvious.

"I shouldn't have to sign up for the draft," I told him, trying to sound as if I was sure he and I would be on the same page as soon as he heard me out. "I'm 6-feet-9, which is over the military height limit. The Army doesn't want this tall a target, do they?"

He gave me a blank glance and said in a soulless monotone, "Get your Black ass over in that line and sign up just like the rest of 'em." And with that, he kicked me in the butt, spun me around, and shoved me toward the back of that long line. It couldn't have been more humiliating.

So I moved along and signed up. According to the induction lottery, based on my birthday of November 25, 1951, I was lotto pick 1-A. Just like that, I was drafted into the US Army. This lottery had been established by the US Department of Defense when the draft was implemented. The decision-makers tried to be fair in selecting who would be sent to the war zone by using the draftees' birthdays, and my birthday fell within the parameters they set. It was either go into the US military or hide in Canada like a scared chicken, as many guys my age were doing. Or I could go to jail. To young Black men in America, this became known as the Muhammad Ali Era, when the world-famous boxer chose going to jail over going to Vietnam.

Coach Van Eman had been keeping track of me ever since he first reached out to me, and he found out about a rule change in the military draft. A draftee could choose any branch of the military he wanted, and he told me to choose the National Guard, which came with a six-year-long obligation. But because that commitment was spread out, I could report to the National Guard facility near the University of Arkansas campus one weekend a month and still play basketball for the Razorbacks. (Back then, guys who chose that option were known as "Weekend Warriors.")

I got to finish my senior year at Central High before I had to report for National Guard duty. On the basketball floor, I was averaging 30 points and 20 rebounds a game, made the first-team All-State Missouri, and was voted the top player in the state.

But here I was, faced with the dilemma of going into college and the Army at the same time. Even though most of the schools backed off when they saw my grades, Xavier and Arkansas kept right on recruiting me.

Now a battle ensued between Coach Bob Hopkins at Xavier and Coach Lanny Van Eman at the University of Arkansas. Between my mother's resistance to my moving too far away, my poor grades and literacy problem, and the prospect of possibly being shipped off to Vietnam, it felt like my dream of playing at a Division I school and being noticed by the NBA was slipping away.

In the summer of 1970, Coach Van Eman told my mother that I had to take a college placement test.

"Don't worry, Ms. Tolson," he said. "We'll set all that up for Dean. All he has to do is study and brush up for the test in two weeks and be prepared the best he can."

Mother agreed to it, but I don't know if she fully understood what Coach was saying. She just knew he had to do *something* to get me in, and he seemed to be doing it.

All the while, Coach Hopkins was calling me constantly. I didn't know what to say, so I kept avoiding him.

Coach Van Eman arranged for me to take the ACT and SAT at Rockhurst College. The ACT and SAT were required tests that had to be taken on the same day for me to be admitted into the University of Arkansas. And Rockhurst happened to be only five blocks from our house. In fact, I had played summer pickup games on the Rockhurst campus against players from the Kansas City Kings who were trying to stay in shape.

Coach Van Eman also arranged my military obligations so that I'd be assigned to the Springdale, Arkansas, National Guard Unit Heavy Artillery Division. With my military obligation in place, he then set me up to enroll in summer school in Arkansas, which would ensure that Coach Hopkins wouldn't find me in Kansas City to spirit me away to Xavier University in New Orleans. I was pumped about going to the University of Arkansas on a full athletic scholarship, if only my illiteracy wouldn't stop them from even letting me through the door in the first place.

Two weeks later, it was test time. That morning, Coach Van Eman pulled up to our house at 45th and Prospect in a white Ford station wagon with the red-and-white Arkansas seal on the front door. I ran out and jumped in the car, and he floored it.

"Why the hurry, Coach?" I asked as we roared away.

"I didn't want to confuse your mother."

"About what?"

When we stopped at the first traffic light a couple of blocks from the house, Coach Van Eman looked over his shoulder toward the back seat and said, "You can get up now."

A white boy, 18 years old and about 4'11", popped up from the floorboard in the back seat of Coach's car. His eyeglasses were so thick, they looked like Coke bottle bottoms. He immediately reminded me of Poindexter, the character in the "Felix the Cat" cartoons.

"Who's this, Coach? Your new point guard?"

Coach smiled a little and then answered, "No. Today this young man is going to be Dean Tolson."

"What does that mean?"

"Well . . ." he said, not easily, "he's the one who'll be taking your test this morning."

I was stunned. "Coach, he *ain't* taking my test for me! What's going on, man?"

Coach Van Eman raised his voice for the first time. "Son, look! You can *take* the test, but you can't *pass* the test. So you better think hard and fast, or you won't be attending school anywhere, and you'll never play basketball again in your life." Then he smiled and suggested we have breakfast at IHOP, before he added, "We can discuss this matter further if you like."

I didn't, couldn't say a word. My head was spinning. It was 9:00 a.m., and the test was in two hours. We were cutting it pretty close when we settled into an IHOP booth. I watched Poindexter dive into his stack of pancakes. He was as silent as I was. Maybe he was just along for the pancakes.

Finally Coach hit me with the question I'd been struggling with, very hard.

"So? Are you going to let him take your test for you?"

"Coach, my mother's said it all my life—'Anytime you have to do something sneaky, you're doing something wrong.'"

He narrowed his eyes. "And I'm saying it now—cooperate, or you'll never play basketball again after today."

His words sent a shiver down my spine. I was only 18. Basketball had been my one happy dream; the one thing that had kept me going for as long as I could remember, even when everything else around me was turning to shit; the one thing I was good at and proud of and made me feel like I might matter, maybe even be Wilt Chamberlain for some five-year-old kid someday . . . without it, what kind of life would I have to look forward to? What would I do, or be . . . ? I couldn't imagine it.

I don't know how many minutes went by before I took a deep breath and caved.

"Okay, Coach, I'll let him take the tests."

I knew it was wrong. But on the other hand, how was it any different from the way I'd been passed from one grade to another while everyone pretended not to notice that I was illiterate. Same thing, right?

Coach was thrilled.

"You won't regret this, Dean, I promise. So here's the plan. You'll go into the Rockhurst auditorium and take the last seat on the right side of the double doors. We'll be waiting in the men's bathroom up the hall. You'll see the tests lying face down on the desk. There will be two of them. Turn them over and sign them both. Don't let anyone see you do it, understand? Don't forget to sign *both* of them. Then, after you've signed them, raise your hand and ask the instructor if you may go to the restroom before the tests start."

"Okay, Coach." My voice quivered as I said it.

We left the pancake house and headed for Rockhurst College. Once I got to the auditorium I was a nervous wreck, but I did exactly as Coach instructed. When the tests were signed and I got permission to go to the restroom, I ran out of that auditorium and jetted to the men's room as fast as I could, where Coach and Poindexter were waiting.

Coach asked, "Did you sign both tests?"

"I think so, Coach."

On which Poindexter left, headed for the auditorium, and took my tests for me.

He seemed to be gone forever. While we waited, Coach told me, "Test results won't be back for a couple of weeks. *Do not* mention one word to your mother or anyone else about what we did today. Do I have your word on that?"

"Yes, you do," I promised him. "I swear, not a word."

It would be an easy promise to keep. The last thing I wanted was for Mother or anyone else to know about this. She would have been beyond disappointed in me, after all the core values she'd taught me. Don't lie, don't cheat, don't steal. And in a way, on that day, I'd done them all. I knew they were wrong, but my heart told me to do them anyway. *It was the only way I'd ever be able to play college basketball.* That's all I knew for sure.

It was the spring of 1970 when "I" took those tests, a spring that proved to be my season of success and my season of despair. I wasn't sure which one would prevail in the long run.

Then I was almost murdered.

Gangs were hanging out all over Kansas City. The 27th Street Gang, the 31st Street Gang, the 18th Street Gang, the Valley Boys, and more. If you didn't belong to a gang, you weren't cool. In fact, you were in danger.

Well, one hot day in June, my brothers Brent and Barry and I went to a nearby park to play pickup basketball. As usual, I was the tallest one at the park. After a few games, we noticed a gold 1962 Chevy Impala pulling up on the grass at the edge of the park. For some reason, my brothers and I sensed trouble and exchanged a look, but we kept playing.

Then all of a sudden, five dudes jumped out of the Impala and circled the basketball court. They all had guns, and one of them was showing off a 12-gauge sawed-off shotgun. I was already feeling a jolt of fear in my chest when one of them said, "It's that tall motherfucker right there, man."

I'd seen stuff like this all my life, but this time I was scared to death. I did the only thing I could think of to do—at the top of my lungs I shouted, "There are cops right over there!" and pointed toward the street.

They turned their heads in the direction I pointed, and I took off running in the opposite direction. Just as I'd hoped, it drew their attention away from Brent and Barry.

A couple of seconds later, one of the gangsters hollered, "Shoot that nigga, man! Shoot to kill!" And they began shooting. My brothers hit the ground while I ran toward the Impala and, with one leap, I jumped over it and landed on the other side. The gangbangers shot holes in their own car trying to hit me, but they couldn't get a target on me.

That really pissed them off, and the dude with the shotgun cut loose with both barrels and managed to spray my back with buckshot. Thankfully, I was too far away for the buckshot to hurt me, but that's when I really turned on the jets and hightailed it out of there.

I ran to the corner of the block, cut through yards and narrow alleys, and jumped fences, with dogs barking and snapping at my ankles along the way. Since all five gangsters were chasing me, I felt sure my brothers were safe, but they probably thought I was dead. After literally having to run for my life, I knew I would be, if I didn't get the hell out of Kansas City.

The five gangbangers gave up and headed back to their shot-up car, but there wasn't a doubt in my mind that I hadn't seen the last of them. Why these guys wanted to kill me, I had no idea. Maybe I'd become too big a deal as a basketball player. Maybe it went all the way back to that James Wilcox idiot who got his ass kicked for even thinking I was going to give up my school lunch every day to pay him a "protection fee." Or maybe they'd just been riding around looking for something to do and decided to shoot the tallest Black guy they could find. I didn't know, and at that point, I didn't care. I just wanted to be gone without having to go six feet under to get there.

I called Coach Van Eman and told him about the attempted murder. He listened carefully and then announced, "Dean, you passed the college placement exams. Get down here to Arkansas and enroll in summer school before you actually get yourself killed."

Yes, Dean Tolson, aka Poindexter, had scored very well on both exams, and I was officially accepted to the University of Arkansas thanks to someone else's literacy.

The timing was perfect. Not only was I escaping the violent Kansas City gangs, but I was also escaping the house that Daddy's other ex-wife and his other five kids had just moved into. I was going to be taken care of in Arkansas, with my own place to live, and seven-course meals every single day. And most of all, I was going to play college basketball!

I'd already left when Coach Bob Hopkins went looking for me all over Kansas City. He'd even gone to the house, but Mother told him she didn't know where I was—she was thrilled that I'd chosen Arkansas over New Orleans, and she just wanted him as far away from me as possible so he wouldn't have a chance to try to change my mind. Coach Hopkins had found out how Coach Van Eman had slipped me into the university, and he was upset. He told me when we finally talked that he would have gotten me academic help rather than let me cheat my way into Xavier. I hated that I'd disappointed him, when he'd been so good to me from the day we met, and I sincerely apologized.

But I'd made my decision, I was sticking to it, and I was excited about it. I had no way of knowing that going to Arkansas would change the trajectory of my life forever, but not in the way I thought it would.

Chapter Six

I arrived on the University of Arkansas campus on June 12, 1970. Even though "I'd" passed my entrance exams, Coach Van Eman still needed to convince the university that I could get better grades than the ones I got at Central High. So I followed his program when I got there: Enroll in five classes in summer school, and if I finished with a 2.0 GPA or higher, Arkansas would let me enroll for the fall.

I signed up for Personal Health/Safety, Architecture Lecture, Reading Techniques, Speech, and Beginning Swimming. I know. Pretty lame. But they seemed like the least challenging courses the university had to offer, and even swimming was hard for me, since I couldn't swim.

Somehow I managed to get a C, a D, a B, a B, and a C in those five classes. The coach kept a close eye on my schoolwork and had regular talks with my instructors to make sure no Fs showed up and I'd still be around for the fall semester.

I have to say, going to summer school helped me through the culture shock of moving to Arkansas. I'd never been in classes with white kids in my life, and now I was the only Black kid in my classes in an all-white school in the rural South. I'd played basketball around some white kids in high school, but I never got to know any of them.

The hippie movement was sweeping America at the time, especially at colleges, and the U of A was no exception. White students would sit outside the Student Union with long hair, sandals, and big holes in their jeans. Some of their T-shirts even had marijuana leaves on them. Here I was, 6-feet-9 and Black, not exactly the kind of look that blended in. The students were friendly enough, mostly because I was on the basketball team. But coming from Kansas City, I almost felt like I'd landed on a whole new planet.

Coach Van Eman knew he had his hands full just keeping me in school and on the team. He made sure I was signed up for all my classes. He also arranged with the National Guard that if I had a game or any other kind of basketball conflict, I could make up my one-weekend-a-month obligation on a different weekend. (Even during the Vietnam War, the military treated basketball players as differently as schools did.) In the summer, I would have to report for heavy duty artillery training at the base in Springdale, Arkansas, about 15 miles away from campus.

I took a full 15-hour class load my first semester as a freshman, and it was a disaster. I got a C in Introduction to Education, an A in Team Sports, and another A in Fundamentals of Basketball. But I failed English and Business Management, and I would have failed Math if Coach hadn't begged the professor to up the F to a D.

So out of those 15 hours, I passed 12, dropped three, and got an overall GPA of 1.33. I needed a 2.0 to continue, but Coach Van Eman told me not to worry about it, he would take care of it. Once I made it to the basketball court, my grades didn't seem to matter as much. While playing for the Razorbacks, I set records that still stand to this day. I had a 13.2 rebound average during my career at the U of A that included a 14.7 rebound average in my senior year. No player has broken those records in the 50-plus years since.

With November came the start of the basketball season, and it was my time to shine. To my frustration, the NCAA Rules Committee had ordered the removal of the slam dunk from amateur, high school, and college basketball in 1967, under the theory that dunking gave Black players an unfair advantage over white players. The Razorbacks were honoring the "no dunk rule," which took away a big part of my game. I was convinced that if NBA scouts could see me dunk, I'd have offers to turn pro in no time.

In those days, freshmen couldn't play varsity basketball, we could only play on the freshman team. So the season started with the freshmen and varsity teams playing a Red and White Razorback inter-squad game with about 8,000 fans watching. I scored 32 points and grabbed 29 rebounds against the varsity team. Even though we freshmen lost that game, each squad scored more than 100 points, and suddenly a football-crazed school was beginning to talk about basketball.

My first year, our freshman team record was 16–0. We became the first basketball team in the history of the University of Arkansas to rank in the top 10 among Division I colleges. Nationally, I was the leading rebounder and eighth leading scorer for freshmen, averaging 30 points and 20 rebounds a game—unheard of in those years. As a team, we averaged 104 points and 75 rebounds a game.

The varsity team was a different story. Their record that year was a disastrous 5–21. Fans started coming to freshman games, watching us play, and then leaving Barnhill Arena before the varsity games began. Coach Van Eman would stand by the door and beg the students to stick around, but about half the crowd would take off before the varsity team even took the floor.

After my success on the court my freshman year, I knew it didn't matter what I did in the classroom. They weren't about to let me flunk out. They saw me as the future of University of Arkansas basketball. Coach Van Eman even started proudly introducing me to the school's alumni.

One day he introduced me to an alumnus and team booster named Gus Blass.

"Let's go for a ride," Gus said. I hopped into his car, and off we went to his department store in Little Rock, one of the biggest in Arkansas.

"Dean," he said as we walked inside, "go pick yourself out 10 pairs of slacks, some shirts, a few pairs of shoes, and a few leather coats. When you're done, just take it all to one of the cashiers. I've told them you're coming, and they'll take care of everything."

Unbelievable. But I wasn't about to insult him by turning him down, so I walked around that store, picked out everything he'd specified, and brought it all to a cashier. She removed all the price tags, folded and bagged everything for me, and I was free to leave. I left the store with about $1,000 worth of clothes (almost $7,500 worth today). I felt like royalty.

The boosters knew I was poor. They saw me wearing nothing but T-shirts, jeans, and tennis shoes every day, and they understood how to get my attention. If it wasn't a shopping trip, they'd find other ways to "make friends."

Before games, we'd have receptions for the alumni and boosters, with refreshments provided by the university. Then they'd go to the arena to watch the game, and afterwards some booster would ask me to meet them outside. When I did, they'd make sure no one was around, and then they'd reach into their pocket and slip me a fistful of cash.

"Don't count it here," I remember one booster murmuring the first time I met him. "Wait 'til you get to your dorm room."

Once I got to my room, I'd pull out the $100, $50, and $20 bills those boosters would give me, which usually added up to around $500 or $600. Even when it was less than that, it was always a lot more than the $15-a-month stipend we got from the university to help pay for our laundry.

I didn't get money after every game. And when I did, it would usually be from a different booster. If we won, especially against a good team, I was sure to get invited outside. Boosters who'd given me money always went out of their way to say hello as if we were old friends, so I'd acknowledge them and the "tip" they'd given me without either of us saying it out loud. I knew it wasn't right, but I never turned it down, and the message was clear: If I played well and we won, I was going to get paid.

In January I started my 16 hours of coursework before the season ended in March. My spring semester was a nightmare. I still couldn't read or write, so there was no way I could pass any of the core curriculum courses. My only passing grades were in classes like Ballroom Dancing, Fundamentals of Golf, and Fundamentals of Field Events. I was paying so little attention to the "school" part of school that I even got a D in Coaching Track and Field.

These weren't even real classes, they were "activity classes." For Fundamentals of Golf, for example, they'd take us to the Razorbacks' golf course and teach us how to hit golf balls. Then they'd hand us a written test on the rules of golf. For me, they'd hand me the tests and just say, "Take them home and do the best you can with them."

Even though I was privileged with my own special set of rules, I hated tests, and I didn't want to deal with them. I was so frustrated, I started cheating and skipping classes. I ended up with a 1.813 GPA for the second semester—obviously lower than the required 2.0, which was supposed to make me ineligible to play basketball my sophomore year.

But considering my lifelong experiences with school, with and without Poindexter, I never thought for one second that I'd really end up being declared ineligible. "Don't worry, you'll be on the team next year," Coach Van Eman assured me, and no problem there—I'd had a great freshman season, so worrying about that, especially with him in charge, didn't even occur to me.

As easy as everyone at the university was making it for me, I was still relieved when school was out in May of 1971 and I had three months of no classes to look forward to. What I wasn't looking forward to one bit was that for those same three months, I had to report once a month to my National Guard "weekend warrior" duty. That meant staying in Arkansas for the summer rather than going home to Kansas City. I hated going to Guard duty so much that I even went AWOL a few times. I didn't want to be in the military. I didn't want to go to school. I just wanted to play basketball. But with even a dim possibility that the Armed Forces could get pissed off by my absences and ship me off to Vietnam if I wasn't careful, I had to cooperate as best I could.

I didn't really hang out with anyone from school. No one there was like me at all, and I missed my family. So I brought my brother Brent to Arkansas to spend the summer with me. I took a job cutting grass with the Parks Department in Little Rock, and Brent went to work for a large construction company, framing and building houses. We rented a small house in the inner city, and after work we went all over Little Rock playing basketball, quickly becoming known as "the Tolson Brothers" in the city gyms until it seemed as if everyone in the whole state knew my brother and me. I loved having him with me. Brent wasn't only my brother; he was my best friend.

One day I got bored waiting for him to come home from work, so I decided to go across town and visit a girl I was dating. It was raining, so I threw on my raincoat, ran out the door, and flagged a Yellow Cab.

It was about 6:00 p.m., dreary, wet, and nasty. I jumped into the taxi, gave the driver my girlfriend's address, and off we went. I was watching the rain out the back window when I noticed a big Greyhound bus at the top of the hill behind us, less than a block away. It was coming fast on the slick wet street and swerving, apparently almost out of control as it tried to change lanes to avoid hitting the cab.

I panicked, shouted a warning to the taxi driver, and ducked down between the seats to brace myself for the inevitable crash. The bus was going 50 mph when it collided with the cab's passenger-side rear taillight. The "boom!" was like a bomb had gone off. Glass exploded everywhere while the vehicle was squashed forward all the way to the front seat and the two rear doors sealed completely shut. I was tossed around the back seat, and the driver's head had smashed into the steering wheel by the time the taxi came to a stop on the sidewalk.

I opened my eyes to see that spears of glass were stuck all over my body, and I was bleeding from an artery in my right leg. I was in so much shock that my first thought was, "Am I dying?"

In spite of the excruciating pain I was in, I managed to climb into the front seat, open the passenger door, and drag myself out onto the sidewalk. While crawling over the seat, I looked at the cab driver. He was pinned against the steering wheel, not moving, and I could see his brains leaking through his forehead and skull. I didn't know if he was still alive, but I was too badly injured to help him, even if I'd had a clue what to do.

I was staggering around on the sidewalk, completely disoriented, with blood pouring out of my leg, when a Black man came running out of the bar on the corner a few doors away to see what the hell was going on. He looked at me, then at the taxi driver, then at the bus.

"Sit down, Nigger!" he yelled into my face. "A damned Greyhound bus done hit you! You got money coming!"

I had no idea what the hell he was talking about. There I was, confused and barely conscious, dusted with dirt and glass from head to toe, my leg squirting blood like a horror movie fountain, the poor guy behind the wheel had brains running down his face, and all this drunk could think about is how I can cash in on this nightmare by suing a big company like Greyhound? Seriously?

All I could do was stare at him while he kept repeating, over and over again, "Man, you got big money coming! Wish they'd hit me!"

Finally, a white station-wagon-type ambulance arrived, and two paramedics jumped out. One raced to the taxi driver, and the other one ran to me. He tore my pant leg wide open all the way down to the cuff and told me, "We got to get this bleeding stopped. You've lost a lot of blood."

He opened his emergency kit and pulled out three rolls of white gauze and three rolls of white tape while he talked to himself about whether or not I might have broken bones in my leg. Then he inspected the wound, poured some kind of liquid into the gaping hole, and bandaged it while applying pressure to the artery.

While I was being tended to, I heard the paramedic who was taking care of the cab driver break the news that they could cancel the second ambulance they'd called to take him to the hospital and call the coroner instead. The driver didn't make it. I remember wondering if the poor guy had a family.

Not knowing if I had any broken bones, the paramedics splinted my leg, started to load me into the station-wagon ambulance . . . and, of course, discovered that, with my leg splinted, there was no way I could fit in the back. I was still bleeding, so they had to come up with something fast. And they did—they rolled down the tailgate window and let the foot of my splinted leg hang out, and we were off to the emergency room.

A neighbor, Mr. McFarland, picked me up from the hospital at about one in the morning, and I went home with 35 stitches in my right leg, a slight concussion, and glass cuts all over my body. I'd lost so much blood and was so weak that I could barely stay awake.

Brent couldn't believe his eyes when Mr. McFarland helped his bandaged, torn-up brother into the house. I didn't even have the strength to explain what had happened; I just collapsed on my bed without closing any windows. In Arkansas. In the summer. Leading me to be eaten alive by mosquitoes while I slept and wake up covered with bites.

I expected to feel a little better each day as the next week went along. Instead, I seemed to feel sicker and sicker, but I tried to ignore it and convince myself it was just part of the recovery process. So one morning after Brent left for work, I decided to go to the corner and pick up something to eat. It was 110 degrees outside, and I was soaking wet with sweat the minute I stepped out the door. Then, about halfway to the store, I got cold chills and fainted right in the middle of the street. Luckily, some nice man saw me, stopped his car, dragged me into it, and drove me straight to the hospital.

I was mostly unconscious, but I thought I heard a nurse say, "Stay clear of him." Someone put a mask over my face so I wouldn't breathe on anyone, and they quarantined me. They checked my vital signs, drew blood, and rushed it to the lab to be tested. Between how I felt and how the hospital staff was reacting, it was obvious that something was terribly wrong.

While all that was going on, the hospital contacted Brent, who called Mother, knowing he couldn't handle this emergency on his own. She immediately left work and caught the next bus from Kansas City to Little Rock to be with us. Her first response? She was upset with Coach Van Eman for breaking his promise to take good care of me in Arkansas.

The lab results quickly came back from the lab. The preliminary diagnosis: viral spinal meningitis from the mosquitoes that bit me. It was a roll of the dice whether I'd live or die.

I was dizzy, with blurry vision, and fading in and out of consciousness, when a doctor came to my bedside and gave me my first spinal tap. The diagnosis was confirmed. I had spinal meningitis and had to be put in isolation. No one could physically be in the room with me, and any visitors had to just wave in at me through a glass window.

Someone notified Coach Van Eman, who immediately jumped in his car and made the 200-mile drive from Fayetteville, Arkansas, to the hospital in Little Rock. I vaguely remember seeing his face at the window. He was back at that window a day or two later when Mother arrived, and I had a bedside seat for a lot of yelling in the hallway, and Mother cursing him out and whacking him with her purse for the fact that her son might die, and it was all Coach's fault for not keeping a closer eye on me.

Almost as upset as she was, he reminded her that he didn't exactly have a lot of control over all the Greyhound buses and mosquitoes in town, but she countered with the fact that none of this would have happened if he hadn't lured one of her cubs to Arkansas in the first place.

As the days passed, my condition kept getting worse. Mother stayed in the hospital waiting room, day and night, for two weeks, until she finally had to get a hotel room. My doctor couldn't tell her when or even if he'd be able to find an antidote for the particular viral strain I was suffering from. She was terrified of losing me, and I couldn't be anywhere near her to hold her and assure her that I was fighting as hard as I could.

Her plan, if I did survive, was to immediately pull me out of the University of Arkansas and take me home to Kansas City. But no matter how sick I got, all I thought about was playing basketball again and, in my darkest moments, if maybe my next game would be played among the clouds on the Other Side.

I did have occasional glimmers of hope, though, when my doctor swore to me that he and I weren't giving up, he'd keep giving me spinal taps for as long as it took for him to identify that strain and know exactly what to prescribe to cure me and get me out of there.

The first two spinal taps were excruciating. On the third one, I passed out. I had to be awake for the procedure, but my eyes would roll up into my head every time and hide behind my eyelids.

The spinal tap needle was about five inches long, but on the third spinal tap it seemed to have grown even longer. When the doctor told Mother he'd have to do a fourth one, all those years of her working in a hospital kicked in. She was well aware that there was a high mortality rate among meningitis patients, so she demanded to sit at my bedside and refused to take "no" for an answer. Even when she'd cry nonstop for hours on end, just having her there holding my hand, while I lay there helpless and wasting away, feeling as if there was an alien living inside me and my body didn't even belong to me anymore, comforted me like nothing else could have.

Then came the announcement from my doctor. "One more tap," he said, followed by the usual speech I could have recited right along with him by then. He manipulated me into the weird fetal position that always made me feel vulnerable and scared, during, "You know the drill by now. As before, you'll feel a little prick from the needle when I inject anesthesia into your back. Then we'll put iodine disinfectant around the area of your spinal cord and apply the white sternal surgical mat."

In went the spinal tap needle between the fourth and fifth spinal lumbar disks and on up my spinal cord. Every nerve in my whole body went on high alert, but I couldn't react—as I'd been warned over and over again, one tiny flinch and I could be completely paralyzed from the neck down for the rest of my life.

I could actually feel that needle halfway up my spinal cord. My eyeballs, fingers, tongue, and toes did an involuntary dance. I wanted to faint, but I fought off the urge, and after roughly an hour and a half, the trauma stopped.

The bad news? Still no answer. I needed a *fifth* spinal tap.

I felt wasted, like a discarded scrap of newspaper on a wet street, getting blown into the bowels of a dark alley. In actuality, I was dying. But I scraped together what little was left of my resolve and kept telling myself, "I'm not disposable. I'm not worthless. I'm Dean Tolson, the star of the University of Arkansas basketball team. I can't die. They need me on next year's team. I have to live! I have to play!"

But finally, after the fifth unsuccessful spinal tap, my resolve crashed and burned.

"Mother," I said, "I'm sorry, but I can't take no more. I want this over with. I want this to end. I want to die."

She reached across my hospital bed, held me, and cried out, pleading, "Honey, no, no, no. I won't let you die. I want you to live. I *need* you to live. Please, just one more tap. *Please*."

It was gut-wrenching to watch what this was putting her through, but I couldn't help it anymore. "I can't. I can't do it again, Mother."

She'd been in Little Rock for two and a half months. She'd lost her job as a nurses' aide at Menorah Hospital for being away so long. But that's how she was. She'd sacrifice anything and everything for her kids when we needed her, even if it meant the agony of watching one of us take our last breath. As long as she was alive and able to get there, none of us would ever have to worry about dying alone.

She took a long, deep, thoughtful breath and then moved to sit on the edge of the bed so that she could look right into my eyes.

"Honey, have I ever broken a promise to you in my life?"

I shook my head. No, she hadn't. Not once. And she never would. That's not who she was, and that's how much she loved us.

"I'm going to make another promise to you right now. Take one more tap for me. Please, just one more. And if the doctor don't find what he needs this time, I won't ask you to go through it again. Okay?"

I couldn't refuse her. The truth was, I couldn't refuse myself either. I thought about it for a while to be sure I really meant it and finally agreed to take that sixth spinal tap. But I had to add, "Promise me you won't try to talk me into number seven."

I saw her whole body go weak with relief as she kissed me on the forehead. All she said was, "You got a deal."

That was it. One more unsuccessful tap and I had her permission to pass through the gates of heaven.

When the doctor walked into my hospital room for my sixth and final spinal tap, I was more relaxed than I'd been for any of the previous five. Whichever way this went, I'd never have to do it again. While Mother sat by my bed, deep in prayer, I closed my eyes and held them shut, fully prepared to drift away to the next world.

The doctor tapped my spine. The fluid specimen ran through the long needle and into the little brown jar attached to the needle, and off it went to the lab, where the technicians would look, one more time, for the microbe that seemed to have its heart set on killing me. If they could find it, I'd live. If they couldn't . . .

I don't think my mother and I said a single word to each other as hours ticked by. We just silently hoped and prayed together, and words were too prosaic for what we were feeling in those hours.

The next sound I remember hearing was the squishing noise of a nurse's shoes, running up the hall toward my room. She couldn't even wait until she got there to start shouting, "We found it! We found it! Mr. Tolson, we finally got it!"

Not only had they pinpointed the deadly microbe, but they also had the antibiotics on hand that would cure me.

Tears of joy rolled down my mother's face, and mine.

Somehow, I'd managed to survive.

This was one of those times when survival wasn't enough. I was going to *live*, and I'd be damned if I was going to squander this miraculous gift of life I'd been given.

When I was well enough, I went home to Kansas City to stay with Mother and finish recuperating. She was dead set against my returning to Arkansas. It wasn't easy, but after a lot of long talks, and my reminding her that she didn't raise a quitter, I managed to persuade her to let me finishing playing out my scholarship. She wasn't happy about it, but she couldn't deny the fact that basketball was my first love, whether she understood it or not.

I stayed with Mother in Kansas City for the rest of the summer. Fortunately, she found a job as a home health care aide for the elderly, while I worked hard to recover from everything my body had been through and regain my strength. I couldn't wait to play varsity Division I basketball for the first time in my life and get back to proving that I was good enough to play in the NBA.

But when I got back to Arkansas to start my sophomore year in the fall of 1971, I had a new set of problems. For one thing, the schoolwork was getting even harder. For another thing, before team practice was scheduled to start in November, I heard that the coach was going to "redshirt" me for my sophomore year. That meant I'd sit out that basketball season but still keep that year of eligibility if I wanted to stay at the University for a fifth year.

I confronted Coach Van Eman the minute the rumor got back to me.

"Is it true you're planning to redshirt me?"

"Yes, Dean, I am," he said, unapologetic. "I thought it would be good for you. You can get back to 100 percent health-wise, and you can also bring up your grades."

I didn't make a habit of yelling at him, but I couldn't help myself. "*No way, Coach!*"

He didn't yell back. Actually, he'd probably expected that I wouldn't take this well, and he put his hand on my shoulder. "You're still weak.

You know that. I'm not going to take any chances with your health. And frankly, I'm afraid of your mother jumping all over me again."

I convinced Mother to talk to the coach and tell him I had her permission to play. She did. But she couldn't resist adding, "Nothing else better happen to my son under your watch. If it does, there will be dire consequences."

Coach reluctantly agreed not to redshirt me after all, but as hard as I tried to hide it, I couldn't deny that I wasn't back to normal yet. I'd have dizzy spells, or faint, and I'd have to fall out at practice. Coach Van Eman was watching me like a hawk, and he still wouldn't let me practice at full speed.

At our first game that season, a home game against Georgia Tech, I walked out on the floor for the first time as a Division I varsity player, and the fans gave me a standing ovation. It was incredible. When I looked up, the lights at Barnhill Arena blinded me. I was dizzy, but I managed to stay on my feet. We only lost by five points, but I scored 11 points and had 10 rebounds. A good first showing. Depleted health and all, I finished first in rebounding and second in scoring for the team that season.

I received my grades at the end of my sophomore year. They looked like this:

Art - B

English Composition - D

Individual Sports - B

Fundamentals of Tennis - B

Coaching Basketball - D

General Zoology - D

In the spring of 1972, after one summer school session and four college semesters, my GPA of 1.533 was even further below the 2.0 eligibility average, and that's with the D in English Composition that was a "gift" from the instructor. So were my passing grades in General Zoology, Individual Sports, and Coaching Basketball.

Being high-profile on campus, my academic problems weren't a secret anymore. Coach nicknamed me "Skylark," because when he was giving instructions to other players, I'd be looking up at the ceiling, not paying attention. My teammates would rag on me about my terrible GPA and about skipping classes. I had a standard, pathetic little comeback every time they teased me: "But I'm going to the NBA and you're not, because *you don't got game*!"

The bottom line, though, was that I only had two more years of eligibility to prove to the scouts that I was worthy of playing in the NBA. GPA or no GPA, with my health gradually improving, I thought I had a damned good chance of making it.

In the fall of 1972, the Razorbacks football team was ranked in the top 20 in the nation. The captain and quarterback of the team, Joe Ferguson, was an All-American under head coach Frank Broyles, and Joe was drafted by the Buffalo Bills of the National Football League (NFL). Coach Broyles was one of the most powerful people in Arkansas, and later on he'd become the University of Arkansas's athletic director and have a major impact on my life.

Our school had many great football stars who went on to play professional football. I set my sights on being the first Razorback *basketball* player to go on to play professionally. But there was always that annoying matter of my grades . . .

English Composition II - C

Technical Composition II - withdrawal

Individual Sports - C

Coaching Football - C

Theory & Practice of Gymnastics - D

Political Science - B

Human Anatomy - F

My grade point average was now 1.686. Not even close to a 2.0. I was worried that the university wouldn't let me keep going like this and take away my scholarship. So I started cheating on my tests, unaware that I could get kicked out of school permanently if I got caught.

One day I walked into my human anatomy class to take a test and headed straight for the back of the room to sit where I thought the instructor couldn't see me. I was wearing a long-sleeved shirt to hide the fact that I'd written the answers to all the key questions on my forearms.

The professor passed out the tests. I was all set to go, almost rubbing my hands together. Then I saw the single sentence at the top of the page. I was able to make out just enough of it to feel sick to my stomach:

"Name the 206 bones of the human body, and briefly describe the 354 muscles in one sentence or less that control those bones."

"*Holy shit!*" I muttered under my breath.

After sitting there staring at that test for several minutes, I just wrote my name on it and turned it in.

The professor looked at it and then at me. "Dean, why are you handing me a blank test?"

"I'll just take my F and be done with it, thank you," I told her, and added, "I didn't study for this." No need for her to know I had come fully prepared to cheat, but she just hadn't asked the questions I was ready to answer.

I walked out of the room knowing I'd reached the lowest point of my academic career. I was a fool to think I could cheat my way through college and still graduate.

I was so tired of this. I wasn't at the University of Arkansas to learn about human anatomy and zoology and a bunch of other irrelevant crap that would never matter in my life. I was there to play my ass off on the basketball court for the Razorbacks, get drafted by the NBA, and have the career I'd been dreaming about since I was nine years old. I really resented wasting my time and energy going to these stupid classes and having to stress about my GPA, but if I dropped out now, I'd be giving up on that dream, and there wasn't a chance in hell I was going to let that happen.

I was so relieved when school let out in May and I could head home to Kansas City to spend the summer of 1972 with my mother. I went back to work at the *Kansas City Star* as a copyboy from 6:00 p.m. to 6:00 or 7:00 a.m., except for those weekends when I fulfilled my National Guard duty in Arkansas. My job paid about $10 an hour, so I was making good money.

Those three months went fast. During the day, I worked on my game, getting ready for my junior year with the Razorbacks. I was gaining a regional and national reputation, and my name was showing up in basketball magazines as one of the top NBA draft prospects. I wasn't about to let my team down, or myself, for that matter.

The bus crash did result in a little money—not as much as that drunk guy at the scene of the accident might have expected, but I wasn't about to complain about $5,000 after the lawyers took their share. I spent it on a brand new gold Monte Carlo and added air shocks and wide wheels with chrome spoke baskets all the way around. Then I put four brand new "tennis shoes" on it and rolled back to the University of Arkansas to start the fall semester.

Ever since I started school there, Coach Van Eman would occasionally lend me his car to do errands and drive prospective students around campus. So one day that fall when he offered me his car, I took it (I mean, why put miles on my new car if someone's giving me theirs, right?). I ended up driving it to Little Rock, about 250 miles from the Fayetteville campus.

The next morning, when I returned Coach's car to him, he looked at the odometer and exploded.

"Where in the hell have you been? You put 500 miles on my car in one night?!"

"Just, uh . . . you know, around town."

"Around town my ass. Where have you been?!"

I couldn't bring myself to say "Little Rock," and I obviously couldn't try to run that stupid "around town" excuse past him again either. My silence pissed him off even more.

"Okay. That's it. I'll tell you what—you'll never get my car again."

"No problem, Coach. I don't need it. I got my own car." I smirked at him and walked away. It shouldn't have felt good, but it did.

It wasn't the first time, or even close, that the coach and I had gone around and around. The truth is, I was a hard-head, and I wasn't nearly as respectful to him and to other people as I should have been. And when he nicknamed me "Skylark" and complained about my behavior, I developed a real attitude problem.

Besides, now I had my own car, which made me an even bigger big shot on campus. I was 21, so I could legally drink, and now I didn't have to ask teammates to drive me to the liquor store and buy me alcohol. I could ride around campus burning up gas, drinking beer, smoking weed, and rolling down the window to holler at girls. And because I could, I did. A lot. The next morning, I'd wake up with a hangover, go to breakfast at the Darby Hall athletic training table, skip class, and crawl into bed again.

Coach knew exactly what I was doing, and he started sending assistant coach Boris Malcheski to my room every morning to force me out of bed and try to send me off to class. I'd just wait for him to leave and slide back into bed.

On the plus side, we were still a winning team. We finished that season with a 16–10 record, third in the Southwest Conference. I averaged 17.6 points and 12.4 rebounds a game. If I wasn't scoring, my teammate Martin Terry was. He averaged 28.3 points per game that season. It was his last year. If my strength kept coming back and Coach recruited a few more good players, the Razorbacks could really make a name for ourselves.

Of course, basketball or no basketball, I still had to get to Springdale, Arkansas, once a month to attend National Guard meetings and fulfill my military obligation. Anyone missing a meeting was considered AWOL. I'd had almost two years of these meetings, and I was just plain tired of them. But hey, what else was new?

Then the unbelievable happened.

I walked into a meeting and was greeted by my battery commander, who handed me an envelope. Inside? "Report for active duty basic training at Fort Polk, Louisiana." My active duty papers. The Vietnam War was still raging, and this letter could send me on my way into action.

I broke out in a cold sweat, imagining myself running through the Vietnamese jungle, a 6-feet-9-inch target, ducking behind a banana tree leaf and shooting at Viet Cong soldiers. My official M.O. (mission of operation) would be a cannon operator, firing howitzers, 102-millimeter 109s, 105s, and other heavy artillery weapons.

Even with the Army poised to ambush me at the finish line, I still enrolled in classes for the next semester. In spite of our occasional, uh, differences, Coach Van Eman was proactive with my teachers, and thanks to his efforts, my grades for the fall semester of my junior year were a nice surprise:

Elementary Typing - C

Fundamentals of Football - A

Historical Principles of Physical Education - F

Therapy Recreational Sports - A

Methods & Material Instructions - C

Western Civilization - B

Which added up to a grade point average of 2.214! I exceeded the requisite 2.0 minimum for the first time in three years! I had a renewed gleam of hope in my eye. Maybe I *could* graduate in the next year and a half.

But I was still preoccupied with the stress and fear of getting yanked into the US Army for basic training, getting shipped off to Fort Polk, and maybe having to fight in that awful, deadly war. I needed to concentrate on school.

I couldn't deny that having my own car hadn't helped, and Coach Van Eman had noticed that too. In fact, he'd sat me down one day before that semester started and laid down the law.

"Tree, that Monte Carlo has been nothing but trouble for you since you drove it down here. You were already skipping classes, you don't give a damn about anything but playing basketball, chasing girls, smoking weed, and drinking beer, and having your own car is only making it easier for you to screw up, day after day after day. So here's the deal: You're going to send that car home to your mother, or I'm going to take your scholarship away."

Well, for one thing, I couldn't exactly argue with him, and obviously, losing my scholarship was the last thing I wanted. There was also a secret I'd been keeping from Coach Van Eman—I couldn't keep up with the insurance payments on my car, so I was driving around most of the time with no insurance. Dangerous, right? Against the law, right? And getting busted could end up meaning goodbye NBA, goodbye dream.

So I sent the Monte Carlo home to my mother, where her boyfriend got drunk one night, took the car out, hit someone and totaled the car, and I never saw it again.

In the end, though, somewhere, in the back of my mind, I knew it shouldn't matter as much as it did at the time. I wasn't supposed to spend my time on campus acting like an idiot in my car. I was supposed to be there to learn. I felt like I couldn't, but I also knew I'd never really tried. That's why my peers called me "Dean the Dream." Sadly, my only dream, ever, had been to become a professional basketball player. Not once had I dreamed of graduating from college.

And now that I might be heading to the killing fields, I was mostly just dreaming about survival.

Chapter Seven

On April 9, 1973, I boarded a Greyhound bus in Springdale, Arkansas, headed for Fort Polk, Louisiana. A GI greeted me at the entrance to the base with a sullen, "Welcome to Tiger Land and Miniature Hell."

I was already scared enough, thanks. Like everyone else in the country, I'd seen the news. Soldiers coming home from Vietnam in body bags. Other soldiers still alive with their arms and legs blown off, and physical and emotional wounds that made them totally dependent for the rest of

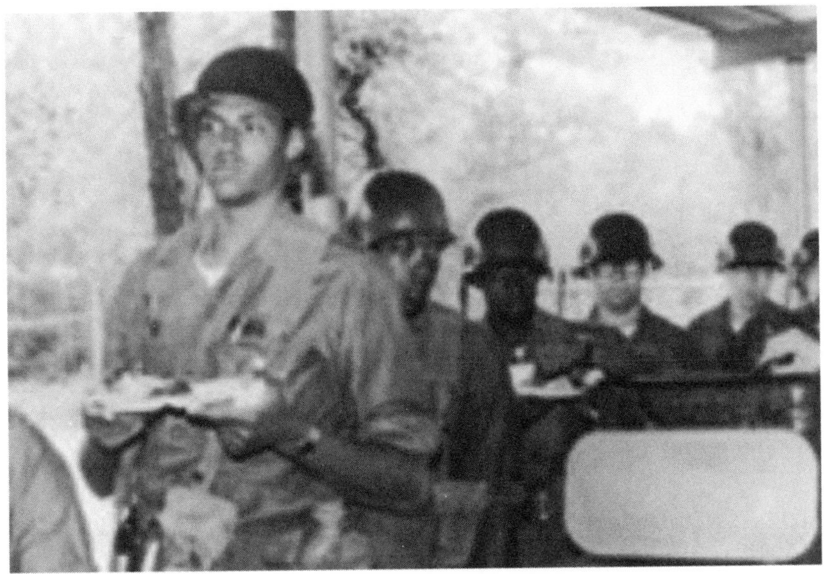

Military chow line
COURTESY OF THE AUTHOR

their lives. I'd yet to meet anyone who came home from the war happy and healthy. I felt like every step I took that day was taking me closer and closer to the edge of a cliff. I wanted to run, but it was too late for that.

As soon as we recruits arrived on base, we were sent directly to our drill sergeant. He was a tall, trim, muscular Black man who wore a flat-brimmed hat pulled down over his forehead so we couldn't see his eyes. He was a 10th-degree black belt in karate, the highest level there was, and he didn't play around.

"I'm going to lay down the hard-and-fast rules for everyone in this platoon," he said when we entered the barracks. "First of all, there's me. Do you know who I am? You'll address me as 'drill sergeant' or 'sir.' But I'm also your mama, your daddy, your sister, your brother, your auntie, your uncle, your girlfriend, for the next 22 weeks of active duty. That means you will pay attention and follow orders, no questions asked. Do you ladies (there were no women in the room, by the way) understand me? Learn this and learn it fast like I did: When you're in the Army, you keep your eyes open and your mouth shut tight at all times or someone will stick something in it."

It was his job, he said, to transform us into soldiers and condition our minds for war. He shouted, he was sarcastic, and he spoke down to us. He was in charge. We would follow orders, because if we didn't follow orders in battle, we could get our fellow soldiers killed. "Kill or be killed," he told us, "so you can *never* afford to panic. That could get everyone in your platoon killed." We had to either like it or get broken and sent home with a dishonorable discharge, and no one wants to be tagged with that stigma. We had to learn to stay cool, think smart, and move quickly if we wanted to survive.

"You'll be woken up every morning at 0300 hours to shit, shower, shave, and make your bed. And that blanket better be so tight that when I toss an American quarter on it, that quarter bounces up high enough that I can catch it in my hand."

I wasn't the only recruit in that room who was intimidated and downright scared—you could have heard a pin drop as he kept going.

"Now, listen up, girls. Someone will pull guard duty every night at the barracks. If you get caught sleeping on guard duty, you'll get an Article

15 under the United States Military Code of Conduct. That means punishment, and you're looking at the commander who decides what that punishment will be. In other words, fall asleep on guard duty and life as you know it will come to an abrupt end."

In other words, that first GI wasn't kidding when he welcomed us to "miniature hell."

The next day we were presented with what I assume were our housewarming gifts: a duffel bag, four sets of fatigues, an entrenching tool, tent half, tent poles, mess kit, two pair of boots, socks, T-shirts, underwear, long johns, belt and buckle, a hat, and a "steel pot," aka a military helmet. Then, new belongings in hand, we returned to the barracks and got in formation, where our drill sergeant took his tough-guy stance in front of us and shouted our orders for the morning.

"Okay, take off your clothes. Ain't no girls in here. Strip. *Now*!" Then he instructed us to put on each article of clothing, one at a time. First, it was the white briefs, which he called "panties." Next came the white socks, followed by the white T-shirt, green uniform, and finally the boots.

By the time we were dressed, we all had the message, loud and clear—everything had to be done the Army's way, and if you weren't dressed in your designated gear, you were "out of uniform." It was a lot harder for the guys who'd grown up doing whatever the hell they wanted. But I'd been taught by a strict granny, a strict mother, an orphanage director, some school principals, and some coaches all my life that nothing good could come from not following orders.

Next on the drill sergeant's agenda was a trip to the barbershop to get a haircut. I had a big Julius Erving Afro, and I always had my Afro-pick comb in my back pocket to keep it looking good.

I was one of the first GIs in the barber chair. The barber was right there and ready to go. "Son, how would you like your hair styled?"

I was pleasantly surprised that he asked.

"Just shave the split ends off and make it into a nice round ball. Give me a hairline all the way around."

He gave me a crooked grin. "All right," he said. "Here we go."

He clicked on his sheep shears and shaved a wide, scalp-deep path from my forehead to the hairline on the back of my neck. I gaped at my reflection in the mirror in horrified disbelief. As far as I was concerned, I'd just been disfigured. To make things even worse, he let out a roar of laughter at my reaction and added, smirking, "You're in the Army now."

He made me so angry I wanted to punch him. But I didn't even need to look around to realize that it would be a very bad idea, so I sat back and steamed as this man finished dismantling my Afro. Before long, all us trainees had matching bald heads featuring every lump, winkle, and deformity we'd spent years carefully concealing, and by the time we left the barber shop, maybe just to let off steam, we were laughing our asses off at how ridiculous we looked.

Our first meal at the base was a generous helping of "shit on a shingle," a crappy-looking glob of dried mystery meat in beige gravy on toast. It was such a waste of a perfectly good piece of toast, and so nasty, I literally puked. At that moment I would have traded my Monte Carlo, if it still existed, for just one of those University of Arkansas seven-course training table meals.

The hot, rainy, muggy Louisiana weather made our uniforms stick to our skin like glue, but that didn't stop anyone from making us march, and of course the drill sergeant chose me as the designated American flag bearer—at 6-foot-10 (with boots on) I could hold it higher than anyone else. And in the second week, we were marching to and from the firing range. That's where we learned to fire the M16 and the .45-caliber handgun. A GI had to fire his rifle with 75 percent to 80 percent accuracy, equivalent to "marksman" accuracy. The next step up was "sharpshooter" accuracy, and the highest was "expert" accuracy.

If we were getting sent to combat, we needed to learn how to shoot, and many trainees who reached expert level became professional snipers in the war. I only reached sharpshooter level, but I could still blow the hair off a gnat's ass with my M16. Because almost anything could cause the M16s to jam or break, we had to make sure they worked properly. Our lives might depend on it.

After four weeks of training, we had our first military inspection. Every item of clothing had to be folded correctly and placed in our lockers in perfect military order. When they weren't, punishment included extra duty, leaves being cancelled, cleaning the barracks, or working in the mess hall, depending on how the drill sergeant felt about the offending GI.

Because of my height, I had to sleep on two pushed-together barrack beds. I often kicked my toes against the metal rounds at the base of my version of a double bed, and it was so painful I could barely march the next day. But pain or no pain, the routine was always the same: wake up at 3:00 a.m., make both beds, get showered, shaved, and dressed, and be in formation by 4:15. I followed the rules without complaint, since complaining wasn't an option. But I hated it. Every second of every minute of every hour of it. *Hated* it.

The next four weeks of training required firing heavy artillery and maneuvering through an obstacle course. Heavy artillery training meant firing a .50-caliber machine gun used for taking out tanks. We learned to throw hand grenades, and we learned to fire mortars, flamethrowers, flares, and tracer bullets, and shoot sniper fire with the M16 semiautomatic rifle.

The obstacle course featured lots of sand pits, water holes, and mud baths, plus rope- and monkey-bar climbing, bolo-stick fighting, low crawling, and various forms of hand-to-hand exercises. I was an athlete, so I could perform at a high level through this tough training. Every once in a while my meningitis would kick in with a dizzy spell, but there was no doubt about it, I was getting stronger every day. My heart went out to those guys who were overweight—they suffered mightily during those 22 weeks of training. Vietnam was the first full-scale jungle warfare the United States had ever engaged in, so at Fort Polk, we received training based on jungle warfare, which was, to put it mildly, brutal and nasty.

The fifth week, we were shown how to operate and clean the .50-caliber machine gun. It took two soldiers to operate it, and the recoil action was so powerful, it had to be placed on a tripod for support. Sometimes we had to stop in the middle of firing and change the barrel because it warped from the extreme heat. One drill sergeant stepped up to the weapon after it had been fired with a rag in his hand and a cigarette in his mouth. He picked up the gun off the ground, lit his cigarette on the

Military classes
COURTESY OF THE AUTHOR

hot barrel, then wrapped the rag around it, popped out the hot barrel, and replaced it with a cold one—*all in 20 seconds.*

"Don't even think about trying to do that," he warned us. "It took me years to learn it. But in real combat, you'll learn all kinds of things you never believed you could do just to stay alive."

We also learned to fire the M72AS 21mm Trainer System, a light anti-armor weapon (LAW). This was probably the most dangerous lethal weapon in our basic training instruction. Its back-blast alone could kill a man.

Part of the LAW was a two-man-operated antitank weapon that fired a small 21mm rocket. The rockets fired from that launcher cost $2,244.74 per rocket (around $15,000 today), which is why each soldier only fired one twice during basic training. And people wonder why it costs trillions of dollars to fight a war.

When it was my turn to fire on a pile of old wrecked cars, my partner reloaded the weapon and then tapped me on the shoulder to signal that he was clear of the back-blast. I took aim, pulled the trigger, and hit the pile of cars dead center. Three cars flew about 10 feet in the air. Wow, what a weapon! I was amazed at its power, and I wanted to fire it again and again. But I was also blown away by the destructive force it had, and the realization hit me like a bolt of lightning that I was becoming desensitized to the fact that these weapons were built for violence. I was mastering monstrous devices that took lives. And just like that, my enthusiasm for them vanished in the blink of an eye.

Learning to throw hand grenades was another dangerous part of our training. Everything in the Army had a code name or nickname. A hand grenade was called a "pineapple" because of its shape. Every grenade has a metal pin ring on top, and once you pull that pin ring and release your grip, you have seven seconds to throw it. A one- or two-second delay could end your life.

Our instructors wanted to see how far and how accurately we trainees could throw a grenade. Eventually, we learned how to fire a grenade from a launcher and use the M2 Flame Thrower—the Mighty Burner, as it was called. The training area had concrete bunkers with a hole in the floor, and a sand pit beneath it. If the grenade slipped out of a trainee's hand, the drill sergeant would race to kick it down the concrete hole in the floor before it exploded. And if anyone made a mistake, the drill sergeant would urgently holler over the loudspeaker, "Fire in the hole!" That cued everyone throwing grenades to immediately take cover. If we didn't move fast, we could get nailed with a flying piece of scrap metal.

Learning to kill people was offensive to every bone in my body. It made me sick to think I might have to do this one day, and the more weapons we learned to master, the more desperately I wanted out of the military. It was tearing me apart, and I had no one to talk to about it. I imagine there were other guys who felt exactly the same way, but none of us wanted to take a chance on confiding in the wrong person and ending up in a world of trouble.

About halfway through basic training, we finally had our first off-post leave to look forward to. But before we could go, everything had to be put in perfect order in and around the barracks. We scrubbed the latrines, the bunks, the windows, the floors, anything in our vicinity. My assignment was to clean and polish the floor in our barracks until it looked like "a diamond shining in a goat's ass," as our drill sergeant colorfully put it.

I'll never forget the Black guy from Chicago who was lying on top of one of the bunk beds enjoying a cigarette while I'd been working on that floor for hours. I was getting ready to wax it when I first noticed him and the fact that he was flicking ashes onto "my" floor, so that places I'd already shined looked smudged and foggy.

I didn't say a word, yet. I just went over by the big shot's bunk and started polishing the floor a foot or two away. When he flicked his ashes down in front of the buffer pads on my heavy-duty mop and confirmed that he was doing this deliberately, I confronted him.

"Look, Bucko, I'm trying to make leave so I can take a break off-post after 11 miserable weeks of training. Don't flick any more ashes on this floor, or it's on. Do you understand me?"

He kind of looked at me, shrugged his shoulders, took another drag off his cigarette, snorted, "Whatever, man," and flicked his ashes again.

"I'm not telling you no more," I growled back. "No more ashes on my floor. I mean that shit."

He thought I was playing and did it again. So I pretended to ignore him, started buffing the floor along the base of his bunk bed, and, in a sudden move, snatched his ass and the mattress down onto the floor. Then I pounced on top of him and started knocking knots all over his bald head.

That chicken-shit badass didn't know what hit him. I'd grown up fighting in Kansas City. I sure as hell wasn't afraid of fighting in Louisiana. And that's how I finally got that floor to shine—his butt worked like a charm.

Most GIs who got off post on their first leave aimed to get laid. They went to find prostitutes in a nearby town named Leesville, Louisiana, also known as "Diseaseville." They'd get drunk, get rolled for their paychecks, or return to base with a venereal disease. Or they'd get in a poker game thinking they'd double their money and then lose it all. Maybe a guy would follow a girl up to her hotel room, she'd invite him in, and then a tough guy would step out from behind the door, club him over the head, take his wallet, and leave him lying there unconscious.

A few GIs didn't report back to the base for their second 11 weeks of boot camp—a criminal offense. Going AWOL like that came with a stiff punishment and penalties. First, the military would turn their names over to a US marshal to hunt them down and deliver them back to the base, where they could face an Article 15 infringement that might land them in the stockade. They could also be recycled, depending on how they went AWOL and what they did while they were gone. Being recycled meant failing basic training and having to do the 22 weeks of combat training all over again, and the word *nightmare* couldn't begin to cover that.

Still, anything some GIs could do to get out of their training, they'd do—if they could get away with it.

Our next training courses consisted of learning CS gas, poison darts, Agent Orange, spike pits, snares and traps, foxholes, Viet Cong tunnel rats, and battle simulation tactics. I never thought I'd ever see grown men crying out, "I want to go back home to Mama!" As for me, when I was nine years old, I'd already seen my first dead man, a guy who was shot in the head and lying on his front porch. I'd toughed it out in an orphan home for five years with kids who gave as good as they got. I'd seen my share of gang violence, and the 1968 riots. That's how I knew I could get through the rest of Tiger Land and graduate. The alternative was a dishonorable discharge, which would leave me with no future at all. The NBA would never want me, not in a million years, nor would anyone else. In America, a dishonorable discharge is worse than a felony. Unpatriotic. Shameful, especially in the middle of a terrible war. I still hated the Army, even though, in the end, it shined me up like my diamond floors. I'd been through too much to blow it now, no matter how tempting it was, especially when the final stage came along—prisoner of war (POW) survival training.

About 150 troops in my company gathered on the bleachers to be briefed by the drill sergeant about survival skills. I sat next to a GI friend, Judge Myhand from Brundidge, Alabama, who had a body like a brick house. Nobody in the company messed with "The Judge."

During the briefing, we couldn't help but notice a white bunny rabbit with red eyes hopping around on the table in front of the drill sergeant. Finally Judge called out, "What's that white rabbit for?"

The drill sergeant stopped in mid-sentence and angrily scanned the bleachers. "Who asked that question? Whoever interrupted me better speak up now."

A fat little white GI spoke up. "Judge asked that question, Drill Sergeant."

"Well, get right up here, Judge," he ordered. "In a few minutes I'm going to show you what we'll do with this little white bunny rabbit."

He continued his lecture and then, in a quick, unexpected move, he grabbed the bunny by its ears, whipped out his buck knife, and slit the rabbit's throat down to the jugular vein. Then he snapped its head back and started to drain the blood into a tin cup on the table. Calm as could be, he set it in the hot sun, and we watched in silence while the blood coagulated like Jell-O.

I was sick to my stomach. I'm sure I wasn't the only one.

Next, the drill sergeant reached his hand into the cup and scooped out a mucky-looking glob of blood.

"Come a little closer, Judge," he ordered.

Judge was visibly uneasy, but he did as he was told.

"Now open your mouth."

Judge looked horrified. "You ain't puttin' that rabbit blood in my mouth!"

The drill sergeant's hand flicked forward like a striking snake and shoved a globule of rabbit blood into Judge's mouth. Judge tried to spit it out, but the drill sergeant grabbed his neck and forced him to swallow.

"Troops, look carefully now!" the drill sergeant barked, ignoring how hard Judge was struggling not to throw up. "This is survival! This is your life, and this is what you have to do to live in battle!" Then the drill sergeant reached into the cup, scooped up another gob of blood, and ate it himself.

We all stared, empty-eyed and silent.

"You guys think you're going to build a nice bonfire, roast a little rabbit, and let the enemy know your location so they can kill you? Come on, people, this is real! You have to learn how to stay alive in war!"

Before heading back to the barracks, Judge got up out of his seat, went over to the fat white GI, and slapped the hell out of him. When we got back to the base, he kicked his ass again. One thought kept echoing in my head: *Keep your ears open and your mouth shut.*

Then came the time for our POW bivouac-camping, survival-training mission, where we'd also be taking on an obstacle course sprinkled with booby traps—the final leg of our 22 weeks of basic training.

We were ordered not to put food in our duffel bags as we packed them—we'd be sleeping outdoors and hunting and trapping for a week. Sorry, but I wasn't about to starve. I was a big boy, and a big boy's gotta eat. So the day we left for POW camp, I went to the PX and bought chocolate chip cookies, canned Vienna sausage, potato chips, candy, and other goodies I could stuff into my duffel bag.

Each of us had a "tent buddy" who carried two tent poles, an "entrenching tool" (also known as a shovel), a change of clothes, a mess kit, and a tent half. When it was time to sleep, one tent buddy put his two poles in the ground, and so did the other. Each person took a tent half, stretched it over, and tied it down.

The first night, we turned in early. It was raining, and we wanted to pitch our tents before the ground got too wet. At 6:00 p.m., the drill sergeant called out, "Nighty-night, girls, sleep tight."

We used our duffel bags for pillows, which worked out perfectly for me, since my secret stash of rations was at the top of mine. As my tent buddy slept, I munched on cookies before falling asleep. Strangely, I kept hearing scratching noises around my "pillow." It was obvious that my roomie was helping himself to a snack. I looked over to where he was lying, but I couldn't see anything in the dark. Finally, around 3:00 a.m., I got tired of the noises and grumbled, "Hey, man, quit digging around in my duffel bag. If you want something to eat, just ask me."

At that moment something jumped in my face and showed me a mouthful of razor-sharp teeth. *Holy Jesus*!

I leapt up and took off, accidentally pulling the tent and its poles out of the ground on my way the hell out of there into the pitch black rain. I then ran into a tree, which knocked me flat on my back and almost knocked me out. There I was, sitting in the rain, dizzy, heart still beating out of my chest, a few yards away from Roomie, who was also sitting in the rain by the tent I'd managed to collapse. And next to him was a huge, happy raccoon, munching away on my chocolate chip cookies and the can of Vienna sausage he'd managed to open.

Boy, was I in big trouble.

Sure enough, the next morning while we were in formation, the drill sergeant shouted, "Private Tolson First Class, front and center!"

I fell out of formation and trudged in front of the platoon, bracing myself as best I could for what was obviously coming.

"You were instructed not to bring food to POW camp, am I right?"

I nodded. "Sir, yes sir!"

"Well, we always get at least one dumb one, and you're it."

"Yes, sir!"

"In case you didn't know, animals out here in the wilderness are always looking for food to survive. How about your tent buddy? I bet he just loved sleeping out in the rain with the raccoons." I honestly felt bad about that, but I knew better than to interrupt. "You know, we've got a nice little punishment for idiots like you who can't follow orders. If you don't follow orders in the military, you get men killed. Is that understood?"

"Sir, yes sir!"

"Do you want to be court-martialed?"

"Sir, no sir!"

He let me off easier than I was expecting. As punishment, for one week I had to carry a 75-pound rock with a dunce hat painted on it. That rock felt heavier and heavier as the week went on, but I kept trying to remind myself that it was a great way to keep building my strength for when I woke up from that nightmare and finally got to be a Razorback again where I belonged.

Somehow I made it through POW camp, all of it, and made Private Second Class. We received our completion-of-training medals and were deemed ready to go on to Advanced Infantry Training (AIT). Eventually I'd be assigned to heavy artillery at Fort Sill, Oklahoma.

But for now, I couldn't wait to get out of Tiger Land Miniature Hell and play my senior season at the University of Arkansas and finally, please, Lord, blow those NBA scouts away.

Chapter Eight

I was so happy to be back in Arkansas from basic training I was almost in tears. No more three-mile marches in the hot, muggy Louisiana sun. No more being trained to kill people. No more Army slop three meals a day. No more . . . any of it. I was so done with the Army that when I started my senior year at the University of Arkansas, I basically went AWOL by not showing up for Reserve Duty every month. Eventually, the marshals contacted Coach Van Eman and told him I needed to start reporting again or they would come arrest me. Coach passed the message along to me, so I started reporting again.

But I resented every minute of it, just like I resented having to go to classes. The Army was a distraction. School was a distraction—I wasn't going to pass anyway, or graduate, so what was the point? I had one focus and *only* one focus: This was my senior year, and my last chance to get noticed by NBA scouts.

I had high expectations for the Razorbacks. We'd gone from an 8–18 record in my sophomore season to 16–10 in my junior year, one of the best seasons in Arkansas basketball history. But my teammate Martin Terry, one of our leading scorers, left after my junior season. I trusted Coach Van Eman to bring in some new players to help us win, and my back was finally getting stronger after my meningitis nightmare. I was only playing at about 85 percent of my ability, but I could still run and jump better than any big man I'd be facing on the court.

The opening game of the season was exactly what I imagined Division I college basketball to be. UCLA, the number one team in the country, opened their season that year by hosting a season opener and a four-team tournament at the Pauley Pavilion. They'd just won their

College game, 1971
COURTESY OF THE AUTHOR

Battling Bill Walton
COURTESY OF THE AUTHOR

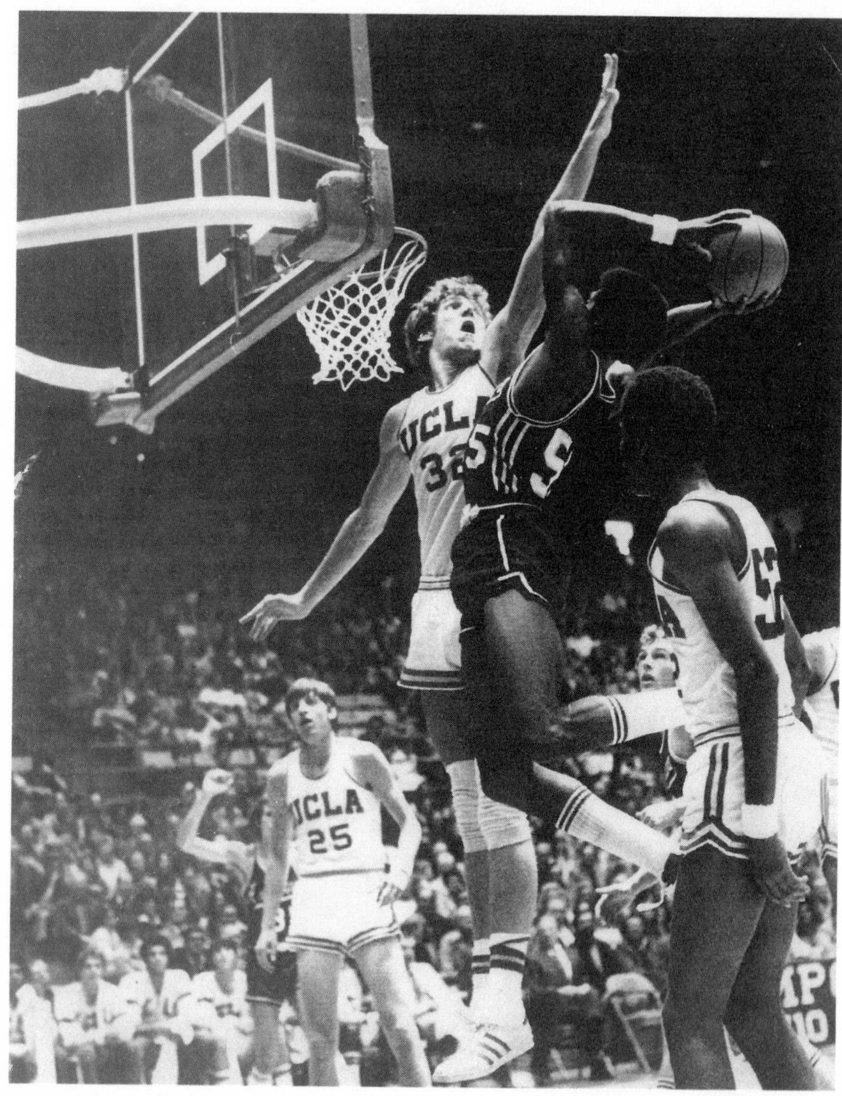

Battling Bill Walton vs. UCLA
COURTESY OF THE AUTHOR

seventh straight NCAA championship the previous year. They were on a 75-game winning streak. Their center, Bill Walton, was highly touted as the likely number one pick in the NBA draft at the end of the season. I wanted to come roaring onto the court and leave no doubt in anyone's mind that I belonged at the top of the draft boards.

Pauley Pavilion was packed with more than 12,000 fans that Friday night in November. I remember being in the layup line and looking over to the sidelines, where Hall of Fame coach John Wooden was talking to the referees almost like they were his kids. I could see it now—once the game started, there wasn't a chance in hell the Razorbacks were going to get a borderline call against big, bad UCLA.

There were taller guys than me on the team, but Coach Van Eman played me at center. I was 6-feet-9. I could out-run and out-jump the roof off of Pauley Pavilion, and he still insisted on having me guard 7-footers like Walton.

From the opening jump ball on, every time I touched the ball, I was instantly surrounded by three players—Bill Walton, Jamaal Wilkes, and Dave Meyers, three guys who would all go on to successful NBA careers. They weren't about to let me score. They'd rather have the ball in the hands of any Razorback but me.

We lost that game by 22 points. It was obvious that the new players Coach Van Eman had drafted weren't going to help us win, but I wasn't about to let them stop me. For the rest of the season, I went all out to record the best statistics I could for myself. No matter how the team did, win or lose, I made it my business to do whatever it took to get myself noticed.

So after that loss to UCLA, I went on a tear. Against Centenary, with future Hall of Famer Robert Parish at center, I had 28 points and 13 rebounds. I put up 41 points against Indiana State. Against Texas, 29 points and 19 rebounds. Against Rice, 36 points and 20 rebounds, and 19 points and 19 rebounds against Baylor.

Finally, along came the final game of the season, and along with it came two memorable headlines: Not only was it my last game at Arkansas, a home game against Texas A&M, but it was also Coach Van Eman's.

Everyone on campus knew he was getting fired. Three losing seasons in four years was unacceptable to the University of Arkansas and its boosters. The school parked a brand-new white Chevrolet Caprice at the end of the court on full display for the whole game, a gift for Coach Van Eman with a clear message—when this game is over, hop into your shiny new car and floor it out of here.

As for me, I was matched up against a player named Cedric Josephson. I told him before the game, "Sorry, but I'm gonna have to put it on you." When the final buzzer sounded, I had 16 rebounds and 45 points. I set the Arkansas record for most field goals scored in a game, a record that still stands today. For the season, I averaged 13.2 rebounds per game, another school record that still stands 50 years later.

After that season, Arkansas brought in Eddie Sutton as head coach, and he led the program to the Final Four. The school began to recruit such quality future NBA players as Sidney Moncrief, Ron Brewer, and Marvin Delph, who became known as the Three Musketeers. The Razorbacks may not have had the success I hoped we would, but the University of Arkansas was known as a football school before I got there. I'm very proud that I put Razorback basketball on the map. Now if I could just be the first Arkansas player to make it into the NBA. . . .

When the basketball season ended, I stayed on campus to play ball and get ready for the draft. Never picked up a book. Never showed up to class. No one cared about my grades. They never had. Once they'd used me up for my talent on the court, I was a ghost. One of my coaches would at least give me the key to the gym so I could practice and stay at the top of my game for the pros.

Enter Bob Hopkins back into my life, the coach who'd wanted me to play for Xavier. He reached out to me. He still believed I was the best high school player he'd ever seen, he told me, and he had major news—he was joining the coaching staff of the Seattle SuperSonics, and he wanted me to know that if all went according to plan, I'd be drafted in the second round by the team. It took me days, maybe weeks, to convince myself I hadn't just dreamed that phone call.

The NBA draft took place on May 28, 1974, in New York City. It wasn't the fancy televised event it is now. It happened on a Tuesday afternoon, and most of the players weren't even there.

I was back home in Kansas City, working part-time at the *Kansas City Star*. I was glued to the teletype machine as the draft picks were announced, and finally, there it was: Seattle SuperSonics. Second round pick . . . I held my breath, braced for the thrill of reading my name . . . Leonard Gray, Long Beach State! Wait, what? I knew about Leonard Gray, another player from the Kansas area Coach Hopkins had followed.

I was still regrouping from the disappointment, still keeping an eye on the teletype, when, like some miracle, my name appeared: "Dean Tolson, 5th round, 80th pick overall, Seattle SuperSonics"!!!

Coach Hopkins told me later that he'd pushed for me, but NBA legend Bill Russell, who was now head coach and general manager of the SuperSonics, didn't trust Coach's judgment and picked Gray instead.

It didn't matter to me. Not one bit. Second round, fifth round, same bottom line—I'd been drafted into the NBA! This was the day I'd been living for since I was nine years old! My mother's words were still ringing in my ears. "All little nappy-headed Black homeboys want to play in the NBA." Well, this little nappy-headed Black boy made it, Mother. Nappy, and natty. Not little anymore. Or a homeboy. Not a bullet dodger, or a car jumper, or a kid taking swats from a high school principal, or a man at death's door, or a soldier lugging around a 75-pound rock for a week because he brought snacks on a camping trip. I was Dean Tolson. Fifth-round pick for the Seattle SuperSonics. The first player in history from Kansas City, Missouri, to be drafted into the NBA. I'd shot for the moon, and instead of falling from the stars in the process, I'd elbowed them out of my way and landed there, safe, sound, and ready for action.

I could see it now—I'd make millions and buy a new house and new cars for me and my mother. Mother could retire and hire her own housekeeper, and my nights as a copyboy would be over with forever. All those girls who turned me down for dates in high school could kiss my ass. And everyone who ever told me I'd never make it without a college degree and kept trying to shove all those useless classes down my throat? Watch me now, fools.

Okay, I admit it, an education would have helped *a lot* when it came to negotiating the politics of the NBA, but who knew politics even existed in professional basketball? Definitely not me, but I learned fast.

In June of 1974, I flew to Seattle. My traveling companion was E. J. Ball, a lawyer from the University of Arkansas who was with me to help negotiate my contract. We were scheduled for a meeting with the legend himself, Bill Russell, the player I'd watched on TV doing battle with Wilt Chamberlain when I was nine years old. Now he was going to be my coach! I couldn't believe it!

I managed to modulate my awe when we walked into Russell's office and introduced ourselves. Then, as soon as we took our seats, Russell let out this high-pitched cackle of a laugh.

"You're stupid!" he snorted, pointing at me. "You're stupid . . . " he repeated, and focused on E. J. Ball, " . . . and *you're* stupid." He turned to me again. "Boy, you don't need anyone to negotiate your contract. I'm paying you minimum wage. Thirty thousand dollars." He pointed at E. J. "And you're going to give this guy 10 percent of that? For what, for sitting here?" And he laughed some more.

I wasn't about to tell him the real reason E. J. was there—I still couldn't read. I didn't want to sign anything that I didn't understand, so E. J. was there to go through the contract with me. I knew there was nothing stupid about that. But as condescending and insulting as Russell had already been in the first two meetings we met, nothing like the friendly Wilt Chamberlain gentleman I was expecting, I could only imagine the howl he'd get out of hearing that I was illiterate.

The first step toward making the team was rookie camp, where the 10 drafted Sonics players came in to scrimmage for the first time. Hopkins also brought in an additional 10 undrafted players, making 20 of us in camp.

I was in basketball heaven—dunking, my specialty, may have been ruled out for college players, but it was perfectly legal for the pros. Finally, I could dunk again, and I was dunking on everyone left and right. No one was safe near the rim when I had the ball. I was quoted as saying, "I'd rather dunk than eat," and I almost wasn't kidding. I was by far the best player in camp, and that included Tom Burleson, the Sonics' center who was a first-round draft pick from North Carolina State.

My performance at rookie camp earned me a spot at veterans' camp in September, where I got to play against the current members of the team. Spencer Haywood, one of the highest paid players in the NBA.

Veterans like Archie Clark and John Brisker. And last but certainly not least, Slick Watts, first introduced to me by Coach Hopkins when I went to New Orleans to see the Xavier campus. The guy I scrimmaged with at the Xavier gymnasium. He got the nickname "Slick" because he was one of the first NBA players with a shaved head. Slick wouldn't just be my SuperSonics teammate; he also became my roommate on road trips.

I learned how to navigate the city that summer, found a place to live, and played pickup basketball wherever I could find it, usually in the college gyms around Seattle. I couldn't afford a car, so I got myself a bicycle to get myself around the city. When the veterans showed up in their fancy cars, they never let me hear the end of my being "the kid on the bicycle," which made me even more determined to show them I wasn't a kid.

And I don't mind saying, I did more than hold my own against the stars of the team. It got to the point where Spencer Haywood asked Coach Russell not to play me during practice because he was afraid I was going to hurt him. The way you get hurt in the NBA is by being late to a play—that's how you get a finger broken or an elbow to the eye socket, and that's why I made sure I was always early to a play. The intimidation and physicality of the game was very different then than it is today, much more rough and tumble. Guys like John Brisker came out of the Eastern League, where in every game guys were literally trying to fight their way back into the NBA or the ABA.

I looked at basketball like it was a martial art. I'm not trying to hurt you. But if you come at me, I'll defend myself, and I'll make you feel it so that you won't try me again. And believe me, the veterans on the team didn't appreciate some fifth-round pick coming in and giving them the business.

Veterans' camp ended with the annual Green and Gold game, where the veterans played the rookies in a scrimmage. NFL legend Jim Brown was there. So was O. J. Simpson. Bill Russell had NFL friends, but he didn't seem to have any NBA friends, which seemed odd to me at the time. I scored 24 points and grabbed 15 rebounds and outplayed almost everyone in the game. Proving once again, I thought, that I'd earned my spot on the team.

So I was completely blindsided when Bob Hopkins came over to me and told me the team was putting me on waivers. That meant the SuperSonics were dropping me from their roster. They had to keep paying me my contract guarantee, but the other NBA teams had 48 hours to hire me and pick up my SuperSonics contract. If that didn't happen, I'd become a free agent.

In other words, my NBA dream was apparently unraveling before it even had a chance to get started. I sat there in the locker room, too stunned to move, until I was the last man there, which is when Coach Russell walked over and sat down beside me.

"Son," he said, "I have a special deal for you. I have 11 no-cut contracts on this team. That means there are only two spots available. The third- and fourth-round draft picks will get those spots right now. But here's what I'm offering. You get on the team bus, go back to Seattle, check back into the motel and wait there for me and the team. You can still practice with us, so don't leave and go home to Kansas City."

I aimed a steady gaze at him and saw he was on the level.

"Coach, I made the team. I outplayed all the players in rookie camp, and I just proved I could outplay the veterans as well. So . . ."

I looked into his eyes. He shook his head, stood up, and said, "I told you my problem, Dean. That's my offer. Take it or leave it."

I suddenly flashed on the moment I signed my contract with him, when he smirked, "You want to play basketball for me, boy? That's pretty funny, skinny as *you* are." Then he burst out laughing. It seemed like I was a joke to him. He had a laugh that was out of this world, a laugh that only spurred me on to hit the floor and show him how I played the game.

I took his offer.

In the next few weeks, Russell allowed me to play at practices with the SuperSonics when they were in town. He'd come up to me and say, "Dean, be patient, I'm working on it, and eventually I'm going to put you on the team."

Then he'd send me out to buy him coffee and doughnuts and his tuna sandwich for lunch . . . and I'd feel my lifelong dream slipping further and further away.

Chapter Nine

Bill Russell had come to Seattle in 1973 as head coach and general manager. The Sonics' owner, Sam Schulman, wanted a big name to help put his new NBA franchise on the map, and he saw Bill Russell and his NBA legend status as the man to do it. Russell asked Schulman for everything, including a huge salary and complete control of the organization. He even demanded that other executives in the Sonics organization be banned from speaking publicly about the team, and Schulman gave Russell everything he asked for.

Russell's mentor and head coach, Red Auerbach of the Boston Celtics, had run a highly structured organization. He'd made Russell a coach in Boston for two reasons: Russell understood Red's philosophy and had the ability to play and coach at the same time, which had never been done in the NBA. But this time around, Russell didn't have himself as a player. He had a new breed of player that was just now coming into the game.

At that time, in the early 1970s, the American Basketball Association (ABA) was in full bloom. The new league, with its three-point shot and slam-dunking players, was introducing professional basketball to cities that couldn't get an NBA team at the time—Denver, San Antonio, Indianapolis, Memphis. Unlike the NBA, the ABA allowed underclassmen to sign contracts before finishing their senior year of college. Hall of Fame players like Julius Erving, George Gervin, and Moses Malone joined the ABA rather than being forced to finish their college careers first. Moses didn't even go to college. He went straight from high school to the ABA. My friend and mentor Warren Jabali played in the ABA as well.

Basketball in the ABA was just beginning to become the high-flying, power-dunking game we know today. But that wasn't the Bill Russell

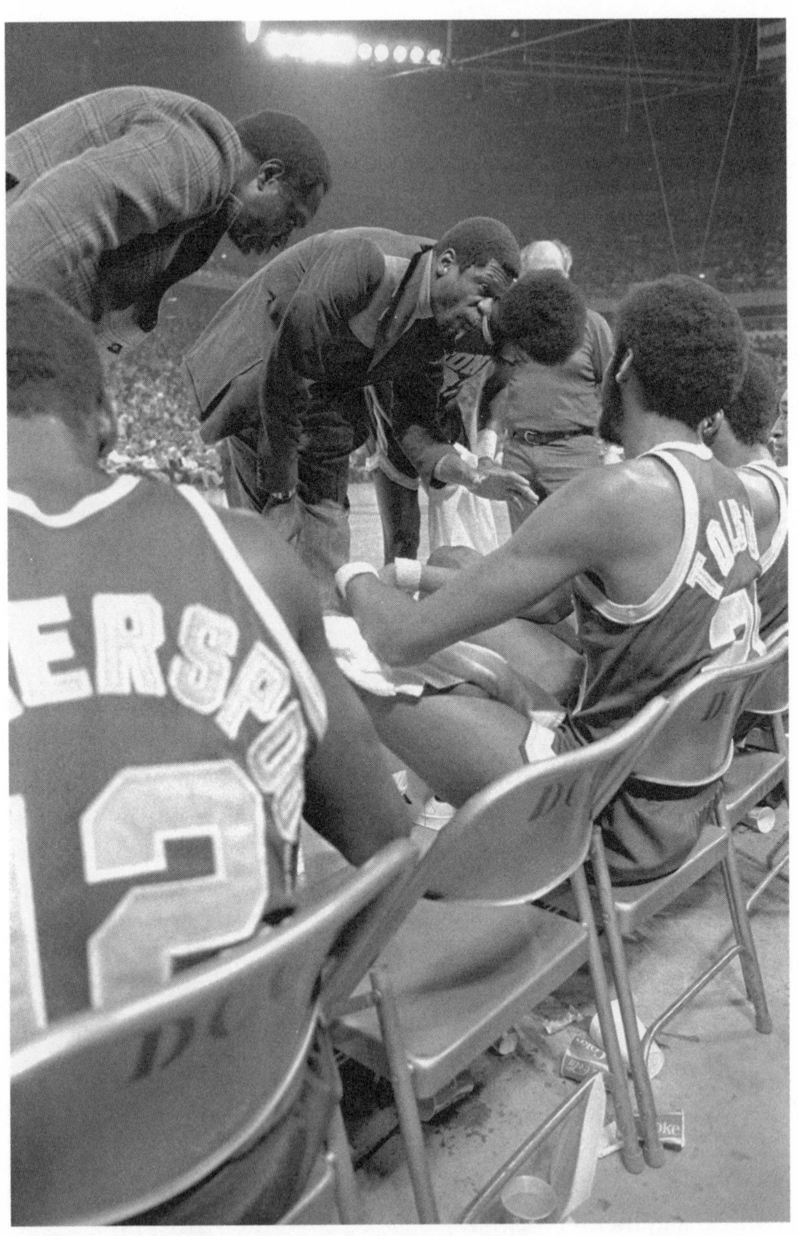

Bill Russell and Assistant Coach Bob Hopkins during a 20-second timeout during a Sonics vs. Denver Nuggets game. Author is seated at right.
GETTY IMAGES

game. He was rooted in the 1950s and 1960s style of basketball he'd played. He believed in calling every play every single time down the court to slow the game down and control every player's movements.

I wasn't a structured kind of player, but I knew how to win games by playing transition basketball—grab the rebound, get it up the floor, and get in a quick shot before the other team could set up their defense. If I could score a basket right away, I'd go for it. Why set up and work hard to get a basket when you can run the other team's players to death with quick breakaways?

Before coming back to Seattle in 1974, the Sonics played 14 exhibition games. Every day while they were off playing those games, I worked on *my* game, and my attitude. If nobody believed in me, I'd believe in myself enough for all of us. And I knew full well that I had someone else in my corner who believed in me too. Coach Hopkins. Which made me even more determined to prove myself.

John Brisker, a 6-feet-5-inch All-Star forward and guard in the ABA, was getting paid big money and had a no-cut contract, and like me, he was at odds with Coach Russell. His issue was his playing time. Brisker wanted to be a starter, but Russell kept him on the bench. Brisker didn't care much for taking orders. He had a reputation in basketball as a guy who would rather punch you in the face than back down. He wasn't the submissive, order-taking kind of player Russell wanted, so it was only a matter of time before he was shipped out of town, even though he'd once scored 47 points in a game for the Sonics. (In March of 1978, Brisker went to Uganda for business, disappeared a month later, and was never seen again. He was legally declared dead in 1985, and it's a popular theory that Ugandan president Idi Amin had him killed.)

On December 25, 1974, after Brisker was shipped out, I got the best Christmas present of my life—Coach Russell named me to the Seattle SuperSonics team. I was thrilled . . . and nervous, even afraid, that I'd mess up and get punished for it. In fact, I was so nervous that I had trouble settling down and playing like I did in high school and college. Bill Russell and Wilt Chamberlain were the two big reasons I'd dreamed about the NBA, and I had a lot to thank Coach Russell for. He'd drafted me out of college, and he'd kept his word about moving me onto the team when a spot became available. Brisker was out, I was in, which made me even more motivated to leave no doubt in Coach Russell's mind that he'd been right to have faith in me.

The first six weeks I was on the roster, I didn't see much playing time. Like most of the 12th men on NBA rosters, I'd just be sent in for a few minutes at the end of games. But then, on February 21, 1975, the Sonics played the Atlanta Hawks at home. During the fourth quarter, our 7'2" center, Tom Burleson, picked up his fifth foul. Coach Russell looked down the bench and yelled, "Dean, get in there for Tommy!"

I ran from the end of the bench so fast, Russell grabbed my arm as I flew past him and jerked me back like a rag doll.

"Hey," he said, "calm down, son. Take your time. Don't be in a hurry out there."

"Right, Coach."

I heard him. At least I thought he did. But we were down 15 points with only four minutes left in the game.

The moment I touched the court floor, I made a steal and took it to the hoop for a slam dunk. Next, I got the rebound after Atlanta missed a shot. Then I streaked down the floor on a fast break and scored on a layup. The next trip down the floor, Spencer Haywood missed a shot, and I tipped it in. After just 30 seconds, the Atlanta players were asking, "Who's checking Tolson?" I looked over to the Atlanta bench and saw Coach Cotton Fitzsimmons get out of his chair, walk toward the score table, and shout defensive instructions to his players. He'd just seen their 15-point lead shrink to nine in 30 seconds. In another 30 seconds, I scored two more baskets and made two free throws. Twelve points in 60 seconds. No other player in NBA history has topped that record.

I ended up with 14 points, and we won the game.

I knew I'd just shown Bill Russell a performance he'd never forget, but I was still nervous when I asked him, "Am I on the team now?"

He gave me a half-smile. "It was a good start, boy."

The next game, I made five out of seven shots for a 10-point total in a loss to Philadelphia. After that, I was back to the end of the bench, playing two minutes a game, if I got into the game at all. No warning, no explanation.

I was back to that hollow feeling in the pit of my stomach. Did I *still* have to prove myself? Apparently so. Whatever Coach Russell's problem was with me—too much attitude, too much desire, different style of play, who knows—I felt he was holding up my success.

The veteran players were no help. They were treating all the rookies like they were putting us through fraternity initiation on a college campus. If the rookies didn't obey the veterans, they'd complain to the coach about an "attitude problem," and the offending rookies would have to run line drills at the next practice. Getting too many complaints could lead to getting kicked off the team, even for rookies with a no-cut contract.

Three weeks later, the Sonics were headed to Kemper Arena to play the Kansas City Kings. I was excited—it would be my first time back in my hometown. Me, the first player ever from Kansas City to take the court in an NBA game. No way would I sit it out on the bench, I was sure of it.

I kicked off that trip by taking my entire family to dinner. There were about 15 of us at the restaurant, and it made me so proud to be able to do that. I also arranged tickets for everyone to come see me play.

The first half, we were leading 58–52. I kept imagining that moment when I'd take off my warmup jacket and hear the Kansas City crowd cheer for their hometown boy as I hit the court.

By the third quarter, we were losing by three points. In the fourth quarter, some of the crowd starting chanting, "We want Dean! We want Dean!" Coach Russell hated that. As the game got closer and closer to the final buzzer, I sat at the end of the bench with a towel over my head so no one would see me crying. But Russell spotted it immediately and yelled, "Tolson, take that damn towel off your head!"

When the final buzzer did sound, I was devastated. Bill Russell knew how important this game was to me, and he couldn't even put me in the game for a single minute.

When the game was over, Mother planted herself over the entryway where the players passed by to the locker room and screamed at Russell, loud enough for the whole arena to hear.

"How dare you not play my son?!"

Russell looked up, startled, saw her, and quickly jogged on into the locker room. Mother wanted to follow him, but the rest of the family stopped her.

When I got to the locker room, the other players were all over me. "Dean! Was that your mother screaming at Coach Russell?!"

That was Mother. She loved me so much, she didn't want to see anyone hurting me. She didn't care who Bill Russell was, or how many championships he'd won. He was messing with one of her cubs, and she wasn't having it.

I'd been looking forward to that game for months. Now I couldn't wait to get out of town, and I was furious with Russell for that.

Emmette Bryant was one of the Sonics' assistant coaches. He'd been Russell's teammate with the Celtics. He scored 20 points in Game 7 of the 1969 finals against the Los Angeles Lakers and helped give Bill Russell his last championship. When we'd be losing games, I could hear Coach Em tell him, "Why don't you give Dean a chance? Maybe his speed can change the complexion of the game." But Russell was stubborn.

At one point, Russell had to miss a few games. Em Bryant took over and actually did something Coach Russell had never done—he actually talked to his players and listened to our input. And what do you know, the Sonics started winning some games. Russell must not have liked it, because he hurried back sooner than expected and immediately returned the team to doing things his way.

At the end of my rookie season, the SuperSonics got into the playoffs for the first time in the franchise's history. In the first round, we played the Detroit Pistons and beat them two games out of three to advance and face the Golden State Warriors. We lost that series 4–3. Golden State advanced to the finals against the Washington Bullets and swept them 4–0.

I barely got on the floor for the entire playoffs.

Amazingly, that year Seattle kept six rookies and cut six veterans, the first time that many rookies stayed on a team in the history of the NBA. They included first-round pick and national champion Tom Burleson of

North Carolina State; my cousin Leonard Gray from Long Beach State; Talvin Skinner from Maryland Eastern Shore; Rod Derline from Seattle University; Wardell Jackson of Ohio State University . . . and Dean Tolson from the Arkansas Razorbacks.

I might not have been in the playoff games for more than a few minutes total, but just for being on the team that made it to the playoffs, I received a $15,000 bonus check, almost as much as my entire year's salary. I took that playoff money and bought myself a brand new, chocolate-brown Mercedes-Benz, just like my friend and mentor's, Warren Jabali. Imagine that. Me, driving around in the car I'd wanted since I was 15 years old.

Not everyone was impressed. Least impressed of all was Coach Bill Russell.

All of a sudden I had the nicest car of anyone on the team. So Coach Russell went to my teammate Slick Watts and said, "Go tell your buddy Tolson, if he doesn't take that car back to the dealership and turn it in, he's off the team."

Slick passed that message on to me.

I was dumbstruck. "What you say, man?"

"Hey, don't get riled at me. Please, man, take the car back and stay on the team."

That was an easy one. "No. I'm not doing it."

I drove that nice car all over Seattle that summer. I was being stubborn as hell, and I also got a reputation for being flashy, which I didn't mind one bit.

One day at practice during that weird summer of 1975, a US marshal found me. There he stood, all brass buttons and belligerence. "I'm here, son," he said, "because you are AWOL from the United States Army."

I let out a loud sigh. *Not this! Dear Lord, please, not this*! "But Officer, I have a contract with the NBA, and that's my first priority."

He grinned and shook his head. He wasn't a large man, but he had a large, uniformed presence as if the entire country was standing right behind him.

"You got that wrong. Your first priority is Uncle Sam. You're AWOL, so you have two choices, Mr. NBA. You can report directly to either Fort Sill, Oklahoma, or the King County jail right here in Seattle. What's it going to be?"

"You mean my NBA career is over?" I could barely get the words out.

"Let's just say it's on hold."

This exchange had attracted my teammates' attention, and they saw me sweating more than I ever had on the court. Finally, unable to think of any way out of this, I replied, very weakly, "Look, Officer, if you'll give me a minute, I'll run home and pack my clothes and meet you back here."

The marshal laughed. "I don't think you understand, Mr. Tolson. You won't be needing any clothes. All you'll be wearing are your Army-issued prison clothes."

Next thing I knew, I was in Fort Sill, Oklahoma, being processed back into the US Military for Advanced Infantry Training.

Weeks later, when I'd completed that training, feeling dead inside, I stood in formation in front of the barracks in the rain, waiting for the colonel to hang the medal I'd earned on my uniform. When he got to me, he stopped, looked me up and down, and said, "At ease, soldier."

Oh, God, what now? Why did he stop at me? I'd done everything they asked me to do. I thought my heart was going to beat right out of my chest.

The colonel turned to an officer beside him. "Lieutenant, who is this soldier?"

"Private First Class Tolson, sir," the lieutenant replied.

"How damn tall is this man?"

"Sir, he is 6 feet, 9 inches—6 feet, 10 inches with his boots on, sir."

The colonel waved his hands at me like one of those *Price Is Right* models. "This soldier looks like Gomer Pyle! His uniform doesn't fit anywhere on his body!" Then he turned to me. "Private Tolson, a man out of uniform has no place in the United States military. Fall out of formation and go to the process center. You need to separate from the US military immediately."

Holy Jesus! After five long years, someone finally noticed that I was too tall to serve! I ran to the process center as fast as I could with my duffel bag on my shoulder and left with an honorable discharge!

As I raced back out of that office, a stiff wind blew all of my military separation papers out of my duffel bag and onto the muddy ground. I was so eager to get the hell out of there that I thought about leaving the papers there in the mud and never looking back. Thankfully, I stopped and picked them up.

Years later, there was a fire at the facility that held my military records, but by then it didn't matter. They'd long since been processed and confirmed my eligibility for military benefits.

I was free!

As it turned out, I was more free than I thought.

I returned to Seattle and discovered that Coach Russell had carried out his threat about the car and cut me from the team. By then, thanks to my involuntary trip to Oklahoma, I was 10 payments behind on my Mercedes, so I bought a tarp and hid it in a friend's garage until further notice.

The NBA was very different back then. Once players were cut from a team and put on waivers, they had to go play in other leagues, or overseas. Teams never signed cut players unless they were superstars. In my case, as far as I was concerned, I was a superstar who never got to play.

Fortunately, my agent Steve Kauffman was on top of the situation and called me to ask, "How would you like to play in the Continental Basketball Association with the Hazleton Bullets?" At that time, the CBA was the league where guys went to play when they were the 13th man on the team. They were good enough to be in the NBA, but their team didn't have a spot for them. There were only 18 NBA teams then. Now there are 30, so I feel safe in saying that every one of the players on those CBA teams would be in the NBA today.

Kauffman told me that Hazleton was "the designated home of the retired Mafia. You'll be playing for Bootie Beltrami, who owns a big coal mine in Pennsylvania. And by the way, Bootie's a personal friend of Muhammad Ali."

I didn't even have to think about it. I might not be playing basketball for Bill Russell anymore, but I wasn't about to stop playing basketball. I was off to Hazleton.

The first thing I did when I got to Pennsylvania was to meet Bootie Beltrami, who was flashing his 20-carat diamond ring. He and I hit it off immediately. He even took me with him in his Learjet, his helicopter, and his limo, which we drove to Deer Lake, where Ali trained for his upcoming heavyweight fights.

I couldn't get over how Ali danced—so light on his feet for such a big solid man. It also fascinated me that Ali's sparring partner wore headgear, but Ali didn't. I finally asked him about it.

"I see your sparring partner isn't allowed to hit you. Why not?"

Ali flashed that world-famous smile and told me, "He can't hit me because I got to keep my face pretty. I only let them hit me when I want them to."

I got such a kick out of that, and the more I watched him, the more I realized that he was exactly what he always said he was—a butterfly that could sting like a bee. I never saw such a tall, muscular man move as if he was weightless. I'll never forget marveling over his speed, his style, and his grace. No wonder he's still thought of as the greatest of all time.

Hazleton was a small mining town in the Lehigh Valley, and most of the people who lived there were hard-working blue-collar coal miners. Bootie allowed me to work for Beltrami Enterprises Coal Mines as well as play on his basketball team. That gave me two salaries, which meant I could afford to keep my Mercedes-Benz and avoid having it repossessed.

There was a general assumption that people in Hazleton who had money were connected to the Mob, because they weren't making all that money in the mines. But there was no way to prove that. All I wanted to do was play basketball and earn money, and Bootie made that happen. He was a good guy to hire me. I believe he sincerely wanted to help get those car payments off my mind so that when I was on the court, I could focus on basketball and live up to his expectations.

I did it, too, and did it well. No problem. That year in the CBA, I averaged 27 points a game and 15 rebounds. The Hazleton Bullets took second place behind the Lancaster Red Roses, the legendary Sonny Hill's gang out of Philadelphia.

And then, believe it or not (I almost didn't)—I got a call from none other than Mr. Bill Russell. He'd heard about my outstanding

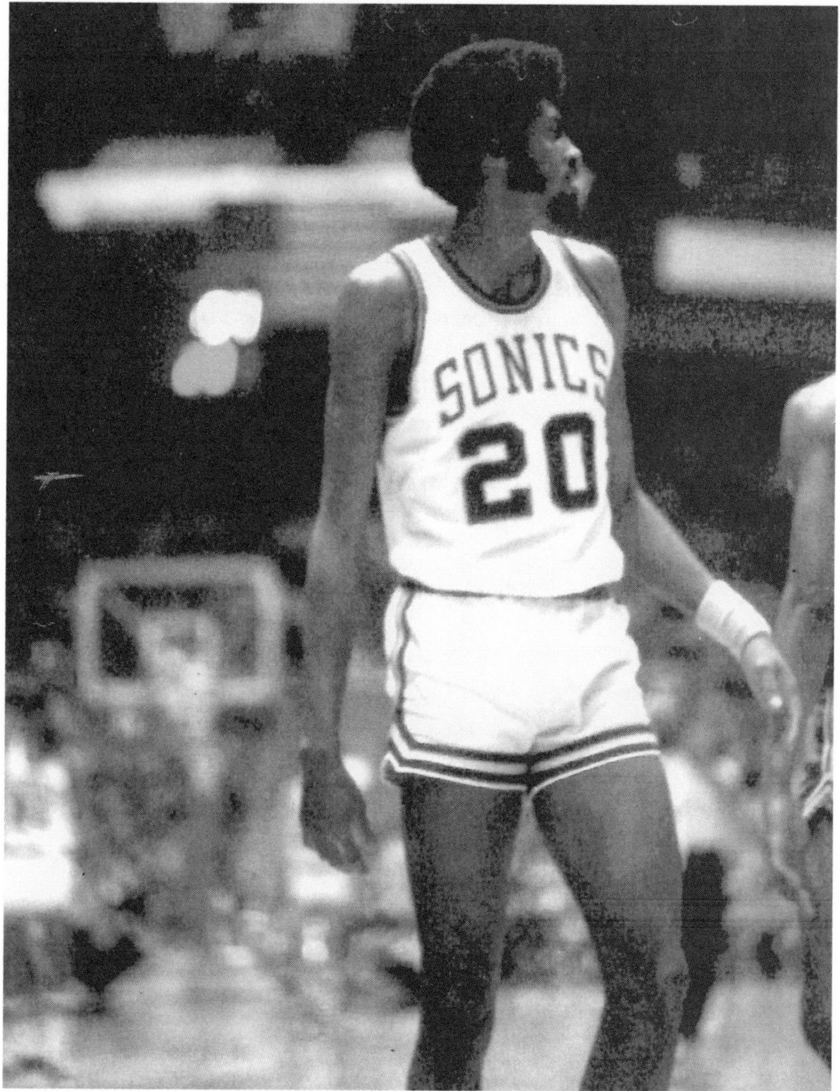

Sonics game during a free throw
COURTESY OF *SPORTS ILLUSTRATED*, REPRINTED WITH PERMISSION

performance in the CBA and wanted me to come back to Seattle for the 1976–77 NBA season. I didn't trust that man as far as I could throw him, but *hell, yes*.

The first thing I did when I arrived in Seattle was head to my friend's garage and break out my Mercedes, now that, thanks to Bootie Beltrami, my payments were completely up to date. Then I drove it straight to Bill Russell's office, where I had a meeting at his request.

"I heard you had a fine season in the CBA, and I want to invite you back to the team," he greeted me as if we were old friends. "But right now, I'd like to ask you to drive me downtown to get my sheepskin coat out of the tailor shop. Can you do that?"

I didn't want him to see the car that had offended him so much. Not yet, at least, until I was officially on the team. But there didn't seem to be any way around it, so I might as well get it over with.

"Sure, Coach, let's go."

So we drove downtown in my chocolate-brown Mercedes-Benz, which he didn't say a word about. When we got to the custom tailor shop, he slid out of the passenger seat smiling, came out of the shop a few minutes later with a big grin on his face, and handed me an envelope.

"Dean, here's a cashier's check for $10,000. You're back on the team this year."

Here he was telling me I was back on the team, but he was still treating me like his errand boy. I looked him dead in the eye and said, "Why should I trust you again, Coach?"

He looked straight back at me. "Dean, I don't admit very often when I'm wrong, but I was wrong for cutting you last year. I'm offering you a place on the team. And I swear to you, you *will* be on the team."

I was in shock. I didn't know what to think, although I did take that $10,000 check.

He smiled. "You'd better be at veterans' camp in November, and don't run off with my money, boy."

Then he let out that big cackling laugh. I felt good. He felt good. Everything looked good . . . for the moment.

I worked out hard with weights that summer, and I worked hard on my game. I attended veterans' camp in November of 1976, and just like Russell promised, I made the team. With my record the previous year with the Hazleton Bullets, my teammates knew I'd earned the right and had the talent to play in the NBA. Plus, I had a great camp and

Jump shot during Sonics game
COURTESY OF *SPORTS ILLUSTRATED*, REPRINTED WITH PERMISSION

exhibition season. Case in point: In the opening game of the season against the Milwaukee Bucks, I played 19 minutes, scored 19 points, and we won the game.

The next game, I finally had the homecoming I dreamed of in Kansas City. Family in the bleachers, crowd cheering me on, and I scored 15 points and 12 rebounds in 15 minutes. Mother even left Bill Russell alone that time around.

After another 19-point game against San Antonio, I became the leading scorer on the team. Bob Blackburn, the Voice of the Sonics, was our team's play-by-play radio announcer. I'll never forget his sitting down beside me on the plane and asking, "Dean, how does it feel to be the Sonics' leading scorer after the first four games of the season?"

"Bob," I told him with a big, proud smile, "it feels so great. I feel like I'm finally a real NBA player."

So imagine my surprise (although shame on me for being surprised at all) when, right after that fourth game, Bill Russell benched me and began cutting my playing time like I was a rookie all over again. Just like last time, no conversation. No warning. Rookie Bobby Wilkerson played an average of 19.9 minutes a game. Rookie Dennis Johnson, 20.6 minutes. Me, only 9.8 minutes, and neither of them could score or rebound like I did.

Somewhere along the way, I realized that Coach Hopkins must have persuaded Russell to hire me, and this was Russell's way of letting him know who was *really* the boss of the Seattle SuperSonics. Coach Russell even came up with a new nickname for me: Scatterass. "Hey, Scatterass," he'd yell during practices, "why are you always running all over the place except for where I want you to be?" I was just doing what I did best, running the floor, rebounding, and scoring points. In the ABA, I would have been an All-Star. In the NBA, playing for a guy whose legacy was made in the 1950s and 1960s with a slow-down style of play, I was foreign to him, a rebel with a mind of my own whose game made no sense to him, no matter how well it worked. I was playing the game 20 years ahead of my time, like Kobe Bryant.

That season was the first year that the NBA initiated the slam dunk contest, trying to duplicate the success of the ABA dunk contest that Julius Erving won in 1976. Each team sent a representative to dunk in three smaller competitions throughout the season, and the finalists would compete at halftime of the NBA finals. Spencer Haywood thought he should go, because he was the star of the team. The guys on the team knew I was a better dunker, so Russell had us compete against each other in practice, and I dusted Spencer.

When I went to compete, we had to do five dunks. I tried much more difficult dunks, and I missed one. The zero I got for that dunk kept me from advancing in the competitions, and Darnell Hillman ended up winning with dunks that couldn't touch mine.

And of course that gave Bill Russell yet another way to make fun of me when I got back to Seattle. "Get under the basket, Scatterass!" He wanted me to haul my ass under the basket and tear up the other team's center, just like he did for all those years.

The game was passing him by before his very eyes, whether he wanted to admit it or not. The NBA even knew we were playing a whole new style of basketball, and that's why they merged with the ABA the very next season—they wanted all those high-flying dunkers under their roof.

I kept reminding myself as best I could that Bill Russell's opinion of me wasn't the be-all and end-all of my career. I knew I could play anywhere, any time, for anyone. I could shoot for the moon and land there no matter how many stars tried to get in my way. Someone, someday, was going to recognize that I could play ball and make good use of me, and if I had to leave Seattle and travel to the ends of the earth to find whoever that was, so be it.

Chapter Ten

I honestly believe that from 1974 through 1977 I was one of the best players on the Seattle SuperSonics. On average, I was delivering almost a point a minute every time I was on the court. But if Seattle fans started chanting for me to play, Coach Russell would summon security, point at the fans who were chanting, and have them either moved or removed for the rest of the game.

As we were preparing for the 1977 season, future Hall of Famer Dennis Johnson and I were putting up the best numbers on the team, so I thought things might be smoothing out again. Russell had kept his promise about bringing me back to the team, but of course, he didn't promise I'd play.

Then I learned how quickly life changes in the NBA.

First, at veterans' camp, I pulled a muscle in my leg.

Second, to my abject shock, Coach Bill Russell decided to retire, and Bob Hopkins took over as head coach of the Sonics.

Coach Hopkins and I had a lot of history between us, and we'd always gotten along well. I couldn't have been happier—I'd finally get a fair chance to play!

But because of my leg injury, I had to sit out 10 games when the 1977 season kicked off. And while I was in the process of healing, Coach Hopkins and the team were losing game after game.

If there was one thing team owner Sam Schulman didn't like, it was losing. When the Sonics' record reached five wins and 17 losses, he got rid of Coach Hopkins . . . along with any chance I had of a future with the Seattle SuperSonics.

Lenny Wilkens took over as the Sonics' new head coach with only five players remaining from the Russell-Hopkins era: Fred Brown, Dennis Johnson, Bruce Seals, Slick Watts, and me.

Wilkens started getting rid of us one by one. I got cut when the NBA suddenly changed the number of players from 12 to 11, and I was always the 11th man on the team. Slick got traded to New Orleans. Bruce got cut at the end of the year. Dennis Johnson lasted another two seasons, made the All-Star team twice, and they shipped him off to Phoenix anyway. Wilkens told anyone who would listen that Dennis had a bad attitude. Mr. Bad Attitude went on to play for the Boston Celtics, won several championships, and was ultimately enshrined in the Naismith Memorial Hall of Fame.

As for me, this marked the fourth and final time I was cut from the Sonics' roster. Coach Hopkins once observed, "Tolson got cut so many times, it's a wonder he hasn't bled to death." Wilkens did choose to keep Al Fleming, a small forward from the University of Arizona who scored 40 points in 20 games that season and never played in the NBA again.

I was let go on November 11, 1977, just 24 days before I'd become vested in my NBA pension. Players needed three years on a team to receive a pension. I had two years, 11 months, and 11 days. I always wondered if they knew how much money they saved by cutting me. Years later I started talking to other players who got cut just short of their pension eligibility. That's how the NBA will do you—they won't spend a dime more than they have to on you, your pension, or your health care. You give your blood, sweat, and tears to the game, but don't hold your breath waiting for so much as a "thank you."

When I was released from the Sonics, I was financially and spiritually broken. But I was lucky enough to be friends with a guy named Harry Alper. Harry owned a travel agency, and his company booked all the commercial flights for the SuperSonic coaches and players when we were on the road. He'd taken a liking to me because I played well and played hard, and he resented the fact that Bill Russell kept refusing to play me. Every time Harry heard something in the Sonics' front office that might benefit me, he'd tell me; and it was thanks to him that I found out the

My house in Bellevue, Washington
COURTESY OF AUTHOR

Sonics owed me $13,000 in severance pay when they released me, according to the contract I'd signed but, of course, was unable to read.

The first year I played for the Sonics, I was making $245 every two weeks. Most of my friends made more than that sweating out a nine-to-five job. I took a good look at my possessions: the house I'd bought for $139,000, the Benz I still owed $7,000 on, and around $50,000 in furniture that was also bought with borrowed money.

I sat looking out the picture window of my house at my beautiful Mercedes-Benz gleaming in the sun, and that's when I finally cried. I knew I was about to lose it, along with everything else I'd worked for. I was 27 years old and unemployed. I couldn't read or write, and I had no skills other than basketball. There was no "next act" of my career waiting for me.

Not long after I was cut for the last time by Seattle, Bill Robinzine, an old friend of mine, began to haunt me. I'd gotten to know Bill when he was a power forward with the Kansas City Kings, and we'd play ball together in Kansas City during the summer. When Bill got cut from his last NBA team, he was found dead sitting in his Mercedes-Benz inside the garage of his house. The suicide note next to him read, "If I can't play in the NBA, then I don't want to live." He died at the age of 29.

Guys like Bill are the stories fans don't see, the great players who gave their whole lives to the game. Traveling on commercial flights at all hours of the day and night with your 6-feet-9-inch body squeezed into a coach seat. Playing hurt, sometimes four games in five nights, because the show must go on and the game is more important than you'll ever be.

And when it ends, it ends quickly. There's no two-weeks' notice, no chance to get your affairs in order. You've got a mortgage because you bought a house where you played and the team told you that you were part of their future? Too bad. Maybe there's a mortgage on the house you bought your mom? Tough. She has to move out, because you have to sell it. Putting your younger brothers and sisters through school? Not anymore.

Some guys are lucky enough to stay in the game as a coach or a broadcaster. But for most of us, it's like we never existed. Once you stop making money for people, you become invisible.

My lifelong dream. A good lesson in "be careful what you wish for."

In December, I managed to convince the Houston Rockets to give me a 20-day tryout with the team. Del Harris was an assistant coach there, and he liked my game. When I went to meet up with them, the team they were about to play came walking into the hotel.

It was the Sonics.

"Dean! What are you doing here?" some of the guys asked.

"I'm here trying out for the Rockets," I told them. Big mistake on my part. I should have learned my lesson from the Army and kept my mouth shut.

Lenny Wilkens and Bob Weiss, two of my former Sonics coaches who'd never liked me, had a talk with Rockets coach Dick Motta, and in a matter of minutes, my tryout for the Rockets was over before it ever started. I never thought the NBA would be an exclusive club that got to pick and choose who got a chance to succeed. I thought the best players could earn their way in. I was so wrong. Coaches never had a bad word to say about each other, but they always had plenty of bad things to say about players who rubbed them the wrong way for whatever reason.

That's the "coaching fraternity" I'd heard about but never believed until I saw it in action.

Drowning in debt with more piling up, I finally called my agent Steve Kauffman. "I'm out of a job, Steve. Seattle cut me again, and Houston didn't even give me a chance. I'm sort of desperate. I'm losing my house, my car, and just about everything else. Anything you can do?"

His answer surprised me—in addition to representing several basketball players, Steve was also serving as the commissioner of the Eastern League, the league I played in for the Hazleton team. During that 1977–78 season, he convinced the league to organize a team in Anchorage, Alaska, to transform it from a bunch of Northeast teams trying to get by into a national league. And he thought it would be a great idea for me to join the new team in Anchorage.

The word *Alaska* gave me chills (pardon the expression). "Steve, that's Eskimo country, right? It ain't the NBA."

"Go up there and play your ass off," he said, "and we'll hope another NBA team picks you up."

"We've been through this before, with the team in Hazleton. It paid so little, I had to double as a coal miner to keep up with my bills, remember?"

He could hear the discouragement in my voice, and he gently switched from "agent" to "friend." "Don't give up, Dean. You gotta keep trying, man."

It was apparently what I needed to hear—I made up my mind right then and there to fly to Anchorage and check it out. The Alaska pipeline was under serious construction, so there'd be money floating around up there. If I could manage not to freeze to death and play my best, *maybe* I could save my house and my car, and *maybe* I could get back in the NBA where I was still sure I belonged. I thanked Steve for his help, took off for Alaska, and met with Rick Smith, general manager of the Anchorage Northern Knights, who immediately sat me down in his office to negotiate a contract.

He kicked off the meeting by asking me how much money I was looking to make. I was starting to feel little glimmers of hope again for the first time in a while, until I wasn't.

"I'll be right up front with you, Dean," he went on before I could answer him. "The highest-paid player we have is Ron Davis, who earns $1,500 a month. The other players are at $750."

So much for hope. "Mr. Smith, I can't come way up here and play for that kind of money. I'll lose my house, I'll lose everything I own. I need around $5,000 a month."

He made a face and looked up at the fluorescent lights before looking back at me, shaking his head. "You're crazy. Nobody gets that."

I literally couldn't afford to back down. "You want me to come up here and play for you and lose my house? Why would I do that?"

He took a very long moment to scratch behind his ear and then slammed his hands down hard on his knees.

"Okay, Dean," he finally said. "I don't want to drive you out of your home, I want you to drive us to the playoffs. I just have to figure out how the hell to pay you."

So now, not only did I become a new star player for the Anchorage Northern Knights, I also became the team's public relations director. When we weren't practicing, I'd travel around in a mobile booth to shopping malls and hand out flyers, trying to sell tickets to the next Knights game. I made $2,500 a month as a player and $2,500 a month as a PR director. The entire budget for Anchorage that season was $300,000, which was almost three times some of the league's other teams' budgets. It was also less than a player like Spencer Haywood was being paid in a single season with the New York Knicks. But hey, none of my business, I was earning money again playing basketball, and I was grateful.

Because the Knights were so far away from the other Eastern League teams, we played all our road games in two trips. We'd fly to Pennsylvania and then take a bus around to different cities from Pennsylvania to Massachusetts, and the local teams would put us up in the cheapest motels in town. When they came to play us, they'd play all their road games against us in one weekend. And believe me, they hated coming to Alaska.

"It's freezing here," they'd say. "We can't even get warmed up!" Duh. It's Alaska.

There wasn't a lot to do in Anchorage, and what fun there was to be had was obviously had indoors. The average temperature was 15

MID-SEASON
Ticket Sale

See all Remaining
Knights Home Games
at Super Savings
15 Games For Only:

General Admission	$ 49.50
Open Reserved.............	$ 79.50
Center Court Club	$115.00

or

Special Family Package Rate

Family General Admission
(Good For: 2 Adults, 2 Children)
$120.00 (add $15 for each additional child)

Type of Ticket(s) Desired ______
Number of Tickets ______ x cost $ ______ = $ ______

CBA Northern Knights action shot
COURTESY OF THE AUTHOR

degrees. The town's arena was the West High School gym, and when the out-of-town teams came to play there, they wouldn't know what hit them. The gym fit approximately 4,000 cowboys who'd spent the day working at the oil refineries, got drunk on their way to the Knights games, and were ready to blow off steam by yelling at anyone and everyone in the arena. Being a referee at a Northern Knights game was a special kind of hell.

I ended up playing the whole season, and the Knights finished with a 27–4 record in the regular season. We lost a tough five-game series to the Lancaster Red Roses in the playoff semifinals. We did become a popular enough attraction, though, that *Sports Illustrated* wrote a whole feature article about us.

That season, I led the league in blocked shots, finished second in steals, and was in the top 10 for scoring and rebounding. Of course, I kept my eye on the Sonics, who made it to the NBA finals before losing to the Washington Bullets. Lenny Wilkens was in full control, so there was no way I'd get invited to their veterans' camp again.

But one day in the summer of 1978, my phone rang, and I answered it to hear, out of nowhere, the familiar voice of my old friend and coach Bob Hopkins. After a few brief pleasantries, he jumped right to the point.

"I've been in touch with Steve Kauffman," he said. "You know, he's a big fan of yours, Dean."

I acknowledged that Steve had always been good to me, but I was pretty sure Coach Hopkins hadn't called just to tell me that. I waited. Next came . . .

"I want to talk to you about the New York Knicks."

Huh? "Okay, what about them?"

"I've just been hired as their assistant coach under Willis Reed, and I want you to come to the Knicks' veterans' camp."

I couldn't believe this. It was a godsend! I only had one question to ask myself: How fast could I pack?

So just a few days later I was in New York, meeting with Coach Reed in his office. "I can give you a contract for the 1978–79 season. It won't be a no-cut contract, but it will be a contract."

Done! I used that contract to set things straight with the bank. I got my house refinanced and paid off the builder. I didn't tell the bank officer it wasn't a no-cut contract, I just told him how much the contract was for. Whether or not I'd be with the Knicks for the whole season to collect it remained to be seen.

And sure enough, I ended up getting cut from the New York Knicks to make room for other forwards who looked like beginners compared to me. John Rudd, who scored three points a game and was out of the league in a year. Glen Gondrezick, who scored five points a game and hung on with the Denver Nuggets for a few more years, a team that notoriously collected white players. The Knicks' white heroes of yesteryear—Bill Bradley, Dave DeBusschere, and Phil Jackson—were all gone now, and there was no way they were going to let me take the place of a white player on the end of the bench and give me a chance to prove myself, no matter how much Coach Hopkins spoke up for me. Later that year, a New York reporter referred to the New York Knickerbockers as the New York Niggerbockers. It's no wonder they wouldn't keep me over a white player.

I went back to Seattle to take care of business, feeling even more hopeless and even more in debt. The power company had turned off my electricity, and I stumbled around my house at night with a flashlight. After a while, I gave up and went to stay with my girlfriend in her house on Capitol Hill.

When no NBA team picked me up, I retrieved my heaviest coat from my closet and went back to Anchorage to play a second season. By now they'd rebranded the league, changing its name from the Eastern League to the Continental Basketball Association (CBA). Steve Kauffman became the league's general counsel, and his deputy, Jim Drucker, became its commissioner. The Knights were still the only CBA team west of Rochester, New York, and we posted a record as successful as the season before.

As badly as I wanted to be back in the NBA, I'll never say I didn't enjoy my time in the CBA. No one was making me walk the ball up and down the court like we were playing in slow motion, or calling me Scatterass while having me run his errands. I was free to be the player I knew I could be, and I saw to it that I made enough dunks to give the fans a good show at every game. The only downsides were the frigid weather and the fact that I still wasn't making enough money to keep up with my bills in Seattle.

When Anchorage made the playoffs, it occurred to me that my contract didn't specify a bonus if we won the championship. I went straight to Rick Smith and told him I wasn't playing in the playoffs for free.

This time Smith couldn't do anything for me. The numbers men had already paid me everything their budget would allow, he said. So I left, and the Anchorage Northern Knights lost the championship to the Rochester Zeniths. For leaving Anchorage, I was rewarded with a new nickname, courtesy of CBA commissioner Jim Drucker—he called me "The International Basketball Vagabond Bandit," a nickname that would stick with me when my future sent me traveling around the globe.

But not until I'd had the honor of meeting Reverend Jesse Jackson and helping lend a hand to a cause that was especially close to my heart.

Chapter Eleven

One of the best things about being an NBA player, and one of the things I missed most about it, was the way kids reacted to meeting us. To kids, we were larger than life. We were Wilt Chamberlain, who made them feel special just by letting them know they were genuinely happy to meet them, maybe even inspiring a lifelong dream for them someday when their dreams were in short supply. We were big deals, the closest they'd ever come in their lives to getting attention from Superman.

Whenever the Sonics asked me to do a kid-centered community event, I showed up for every one of them I possibly could. Teammates like Slick Watts and Bruce Seals and I would have a blast with those kids. I loved spending time with them and always wondered afterwards if they got as much of a charge out of it as I did. But once I was out of the NBA, it felt like that part of my life had come to an end.

Then one day Slick called to invite me to play in a charity game that was being organized by Reverend Jesse Jackson in Memphis, Tennessee, called the Rainbow Classic, to raise funds to help keep inner-city kids in school and find them decent jobs.

Not just "yes," but "yes, please!"

Reverend Jackson had worked with Dr. Martin Luther King Jr., as a member of the Southern Christian Leadership Conference (SCLC). He'd been in Memphis on that dark day, April 4, 1968, when Dr. King was assassinated. After he had a falling-out with the SCLC, Reverend Jackson formed a group called Operation PUSH to advance civil rights causes around the country, so the fact that he was putting together a Rainbow Classic charity basketball game for inner-city kids came as no surprise to me and made me admire him even more than I already had.

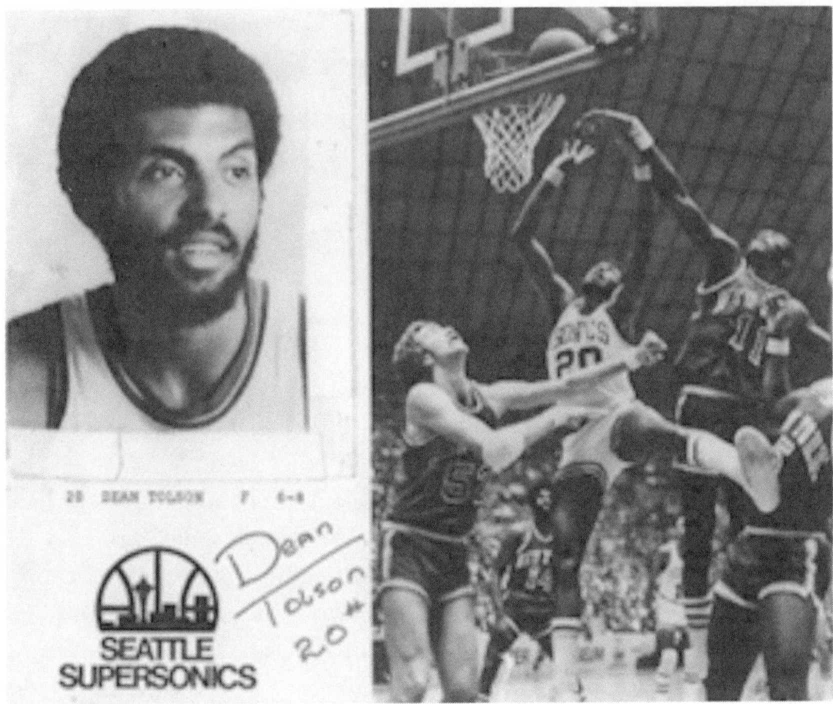

Sonics PR autographed giveaway
COURTESY OF THE AUTHOR

Slick offered to share his room with me at the Holiday Inn Express in Memphis. (*Very* swanky, compared to the NBA standards I remembered.) All I needed to do was bring some basketball gear and my team warmup jacket so they could take a photo of all the players before the game.

"Uh . . . Slick, I don't *have* a team," I reminded him.

"Still got your Sonics jacket?"

"Of course."

"That'll do just fine, Dean. After all, you *earned* that jacket."

So I grabbed my gear and my Sonics jacket and flew to Memphis a day early to check things out.

Reverend Jackson and his right-hand man Bill Cherry picked me up at the airport. Cherry was a big-time promoter who worked with the huge Black performers of the day, like Isaac Hayes, Stevie Wonder, and

Richard Pryor. I was almost as impressed to meet him as I was to meet Jesse Jackson.

They dropped me off at the hotel. I was getting out of the car when Jackson said, almost off-handedly, "Be ready to go in an hour with your basketball gear. We're going to the Memphis state prison."

I froze in place. "We're doing what?"

"We're going to the Memphis state prison. We've heard that the prison is overrun with rats and roaches. The prisoners can't get a decent night's sleep with rats crawling all over them, and we have to do something about it. So we're going to go talk to the warden and play ball with the inmates. I need you there with me. Without an NBA player, they won't let us in."

"Reverend Jackson, I just came down here to play in the Rainbow Classic for the kids," I reminded him. "No one said anything about going to a prison and playing ball against a bunch of inmates. I don't feel comfortable with that."

He looked me right in the eye, straightforward as could be. "If you don't come with us, you're not playing in the game tomorrow. Do you want to play tomorrow, or not?"

I did want to play, very much—not only to support a good cause, but also, to be honest, because there would be coaches there, and I didn't want to pass up another chance to show them what I could do against other NBA players. But when I got back to my room, I had a knot in my stomach. I felt like I was being used. There weren't any other players here yet, so Reverend Jackson, who'd never even met me before, felt perfectly entitled to make a total stranger go with him to visit a prison? Had Bill Russell stamped the words "errand boy" on my forehead without my noticing?

I put on my gear, but as I was going down in the elevator, something was telling me not to go, and I usually listened to my heart about things like this. I could see the lobby from the elevator, and Jesse Jackson was there waiting for me. So when the elevator doors opened on the ground floor, I hightailed it toward the back of the hotel, thinking I'd just disappear for a few hours and come back later when the coast was clear.

I was heaving a sigh of relief as I stepped out the hotel's rear exit . . . and found myself almost face to face with Bill Cherry, who was sitting behind the wheel of Jesse Jackson's car right outside the door, waiting for Jackson and me to come out.

"Hey, Dean!" he called out with a friendly wave. "Hop on in and let's get going."

At that point, sure, what the hell, game over, let's get going. Jackson appeared a minute or two later, and we were off to prison.

Needless to say, it was as grim inside as I'd pictured. I couldn't imagine people living there day after day without going stark raving crazy. After we were searched, we had to move through five locked gates. Every time the gate we entered slammed shut, the next gate would open. It was creepy. Finally a correctional officer escorted us to a tiny, nondescript room that turned out to be the warden's office. The warden was there waiting for us, and he greeted us. Jackson's guys waited outside the office, and the correctional officer left us to talk.

Not more than two minutes later, when it was just Jackson, Bill Cherry, the warden, and me, Jackson grabbed the warden by the collar and pinned him to the wall.

"Listen to me!" he screamed at him. "You need to clean this place up! You have these guys laying on their beds, unable to sleep because they have rats and roaches crawling all over them!"

I couldn't have been more shocked. *What is he doing?! He's going to get us all arrested!* My instincts were right—this was a bad idea.

Jackson kept screaming at the warden for another few minutes, slamming him into the wall a few times to drive home his point. At 6'3", Jackson towered over the guy. He'd just let go of him when one of the guards stuck his head in the door to see what all the commotion was about.

"Everything all right in here?" the guard asked.

The warden nodded yes without a word, and the guard disappeared again and closed the door.

Jackson wasn't finished with the warden yet. "You've got 48 hours to clean this shit up! Now, take us down to the basketball court so we can play ball with the inmates."

Once we'd left the warden's office, Jackson turned to Bill and me. "Sorry you had to see that, but this shit has got to stop."

I was scared and still trying to recover. And enough already with the "Reverend Jackson" thing. I felt as if the past several minutes had moved us past that. "Jesse, man," I said, "I just want to get out of here before they come arrest us."

"You're not leaving until we play the game."

Apparently not.

The guards took us down to the gym and turned on the lights. Even with the lights on, it still seemed dim and depressing—the small windows were way up near the high ceiling. There was a set of bleachers behind one of the baskets, but they were empty. It was after 7:00 p.m., time for the prisoners to be confined to their cells, not in the gym enjoying a basketball game. Only the inmates who were approved to play could join us.

Once the lights were on, you could see roaches everywhere, scurrying across the court. When the inmates filed in, they started dribbling the balls, trying to kill the roaches. Pop, pop, pop—you could hear them being crushed by those balls.

"Man, Jesse, how are we gonna play like this?" I asked.

"Don't worry, they'll all crawl in the cracks now that the lights are on. And now you see why we're here."

No argument there. It was disgusting. Shameful.

After a few minutes, the roaches disappeared, and we started to play. Some of the prisoners were actually pretty decent players. Jesse was pretty good too, better than I expected. And because he and I were a team, I was able to make up the difference, and we won the game, after which he started calling me his "seeing-eye dog."

From then on, he'd say, "Where's my seeing-eye dog? You can see trouble before it happens," and he'd laugh.

The next day, we played in the charity game in front of a packed crowd at the Mid-South Coliseum, where the Memphis State basketball team played. I played 19 minutes in the game and scored 18 points. I was 9 for 9 from the field. I knew I could play with any of these NBA guys, if I could just get the NBA to care again.

I asked Jesse Jackson if, since he knew so many NBA players and coaches, he could help me get to a training camp somewhere. That day after the game, Jesse talked to Al Attles, coach of the Golden State Warriors, who'd been there to see us play.

"He got cut by Seattle, but you saw the game, you saw what he can do out there," Jesse told him.

Attles said he would look into it.

By which he apparently meant, "Dean Tolson will never hear from me or anyone else in the Warriors' organization."

No doubt about it, the coaching fraternity always sticks together. If one coach smears you, another coach isn't going to ignore his advice and override him. Why? Because a coach never knows when another coach might throw him a bone and give him an assistant-coaching position down the road if or when he needs a job. Don't believe me? Look at the NBA's assistant coaches and you'll see former head coaches who've found a way to keep getting paid.

If only it worked like that for former NBA players. But clearly it didn't, and it was finally time to face the fact that it was all over between me and the NBA and come up with some kind of Plan B that would let me keep being the best player I could be and still pay my bills.

Or, in my case, what turned out to be Plan PBA.

Chapter Twelve

On one hand, it was very hard for me to give up once and for all on that NBA dream. But at that point, looking at it from the outside—and I was definitely on the outside—the whole thing seemed like a long con. "Come play here in (fill in name of some small town) for (fill in some small amount of money), and if you break your back and make us great, riches await in the NBA! Simply sell your services to the highest bidder, be your own negotiator, and count on being a pawn in a much bigger game than you thought you were signing on for. If it suits the coaches, they'll cut you off with no explanation, no matter how good you are or how hard you work. If it means blaming you to protect their job . . . well, that's just part of that bigger game we told you about."

In hindsight, it looked more like a nightmare than a dream. But obsessing over it wasn't going to get me any closer to what I really needed: survival. Get to the next contract and the next payday, cover your bills, and let the rest go. "Keep praying, keep playing, and keep paying" became my motto.

And what do you know, my prayers were answered, in the most unexpected way possible, thanks to a basketball buddy named Larry McNeill.

Larry had played center for the Rochester team that won the CBA championship at the end of my previous season in Anchorage. He was third in the league in scoring and blocked shots. During one of our games against Rochester, I'd blocked 12 of Larry's shots and held him to 17 points. No one did that to Larry McNeill, and we came away from that season with a lot of respect for each other.

His call was a big surprise. The reason for it was an even bigger one. In fact, it almost sent me into full-blown shock.

"Hey, man, I just got a gig in the Philippines. They want two Americans on a team in the Philippine Basketball Association. The PBA. I've signed on. Would you like to be the other American?"

The Philippines? What?! But hey, I had my priorities, so . . .

"How much are they paying?"

Larry chuckled and said, "You ready for this? $50,000 for one season."

I almost dropped the phone. "Ready?! Man, I'm already packing!"

First thing the next morning I was on a plane to San Francisco to meet the team's owner, Carlos Palanca III. We met at the St. Francis Hotel, one of the most amazing five-star hotels I'd ever seen, all gleaming white Italian marble, from the floors to the walls to the pillars. The whole place glowed like Zeus's palace.

Mr. Palanca walked into the dining room wearing a very fancy suit, polished shoes, a fat gold Rolex President watch, and diamond rings that blinded me. He introduced himself as we were shown to his table.

"Mr. Dean, I am Carlos Palanca the Third, but if you don't mind, I prefer to be called Honey Boy. I understand you are here to negotiate a contract and play for my team Gilbey's Gin in Manila, is that right?"

We took our seats and ordered coffee. I was too broke to be shy at that point.

"That's exactly why I'm here. I'm about to lose my house in Seattle, and I need a contract generous enough to cover my back payments."

Honey Boy took a sip of his coffee, his eyes never leaving mine. "Tell me how much you need. But I have to tell you, we cannot pay off your house. Now, go on with what you were saying, please."

I knew exactly how much I needed up front to catch up on my 11 missed payments and avoid foreclosure, and that's exactly the amount I quoted.

"I need $15,000, right now."

He smiled. His eyes scanned the room a couple of times, as if he were searching for his response in the white marble corners. After several seconds, he came back to me.

"Well, that's a lot of money. You know how many pesos that is in the Philippines? It could buy a mansion there."

I shrugged. "Unfortunately, not in Seattle, sir."

"Please, just call me Honey Boy."

With that, he clapped his hands twice, loudly, and a well-dressed gentleman appeared through a nearby door. The stranger stepped forward but stayed several feet away, saying nothing, just bowing his head.

Honey Boy spoke to him in a firm, discreet voice. "Go downstairs, get a cashier's check made out to Byron 'Dean' Tolson for $15,000, and give it to Mr. Tolson."

The man left, and Honey Boy turned to me again. "Your contract will be for $50,000 for one season. I will owe you another 35 when you get to the Philippines. Do we have a deal?"

I managed not to go leaping around the room and simply said, "Absolutely." Money aside (as if that were possible), I liked this man. He moved and spoke like a gentleman, with polite authority, completely in control and at ease with everything, including paychecks. I kept silently praying not to wake up from this.

We'd both been serious so far, but I knew the negotiation had ended when he gave me a big smile and said, "Once you arrive in Manila, you will be known as 'Filipino Deano.'"

I laughed. "For $50,000 a season, you can call me anything you want."

Cashier's check in hand, I flew back to Seattle later that day, took care of my financial business, secured the house, packed my things, and caught the next flight to the Philippines.

It was beautiful. Lush tropical green everywhere, and I was gaping around me like a little boy from the moment we deplaned at Manila International Airport. I quickly settled into my room at the Philippine Plaza Hotel and headed off to meet my new Gilbey's Gin team and thank my friend Larry McNeill about a thousand times for making this happen and, in a big way, saving my life, financially and emotionally.

The team practiced for about a week before the PBA season opened—Gilbey's Gin vs. the Toyota Tamaraws. Their star player, a guy

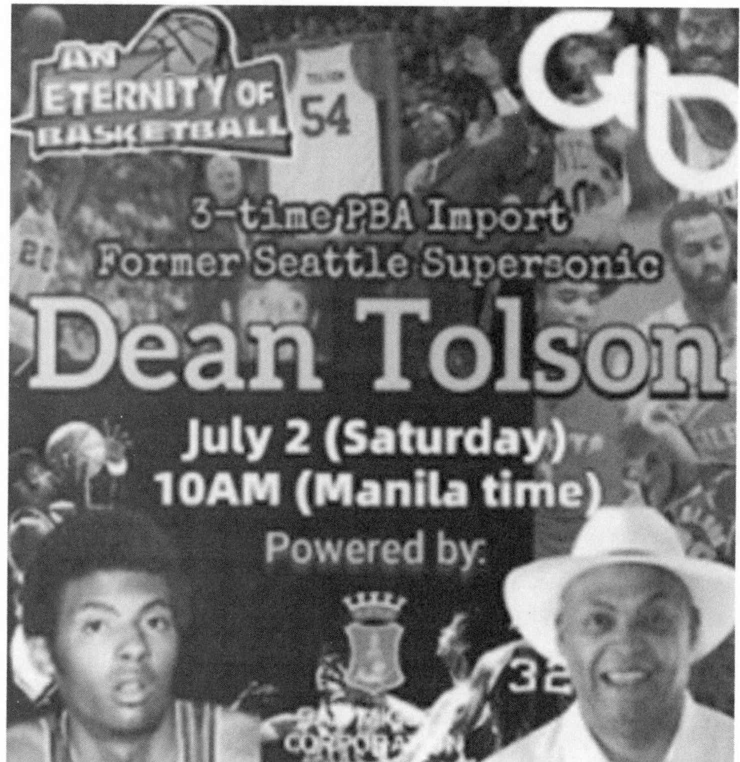

Philippines Basketball Association interview
COURTESY OF THE AUTHOR

named Jaworski, had become a national hero in the Philippines. To me, he was just another basketball player.

The opening game promised to be a real showdown. Araneta Coliseum, the site where Muhammad Ali and Joe Frazier fought the famous "Thrilla in Manila" in 1975, held 30,000 people, and the place was packed for our first game . . . and my own *thrilla*, as it turned out.

Each team had two dominant American players. The rules prevented them from playing more than two of us. The rest of the team was made up of local players. In this league, every team's main strategy was to provoke the Americans and start a fight that would get them kicked out of the game. We were the stars who scored the points and won the games.

If they could get one of us kicked out, the other team had a much better chance of winning. I found that out the hard way.

I was standing near the free throw line, setting a pick for another player that would spring him free for an open shot. Abe King was the defending player. As I screened him off, he doubled up his fist and punched me right in the mouth. A spray of blood went everywhere. I thought I'd lost my teeth.

Larry McNeill flew over to me and wrapped both arms around my waist. "Dean, I ain't gonna let you fight tonight, 'cause we gotta win this game. So just calm yo little ass down and let's play, man."

I did, and I finished the game. Larry scored 50 points and I scored 40, but we lost in double overtime. At the end of the game, the Toyota team was trash-talking us, which revved me up even more than I already was.

I hadn't forgotten about Abe King. So when the commotion died down and the players were filing into their locker rooms, I sneaked down the floor, working my way to Toyota's bench, and stood on one of the folding chairs. When Abe King came along, I made a flying leap, caught him right on the jaw, and dropped him to the floor. That cleared both benches, and a huge fight broke out.

When the Manila police rushed in with their nightsticks, the fight got even crazier, as the huge crowd of fans started swinging at each other all over the place. It was open season after the opening game of the Philippine Basketball Association. To this day, Glenn McDonald, one of the American players who was there that night, says it reminded him of the infamous night in 2004 when Ron Artest of the Indiana Pacers fought in the stands with Detroit Pistons fans. Glenn called it "the original 'Malice at the Palace.'"

To escalate the drama, the police blasted into the locker room and slapped handcuffs on me for starting a riot. Not only was I an International Basketball Vagabond Bandit and Filipino Deano, but I was now also dubbed the Villain of the PBA, as if Abe King had nothing to do with it.

Normally calm Honey Boy was beside himself with anger. He had just given me $15,000 weeks earlier, and here he was shelling out another $10,000 to bail me out of jail. I'd cost him $25,000 so far, after playing a total of one game, and the Filipino authorities wanted to deport me back to the United States.

"What in the hell do you think you're doing?" he screamed at me.

I put a lid on my defensiveness and controlled my voice as best I could. "I don't let anyone punch me in the face and get away with it."

"Well, Mr. Hot Shot, your ass would still be down there in that jail had I not put up the bail money to get you out. I've got my lawyer on this thing. There won't be any more of this kind of stuff, do you understand? I don't have the money, or the time, to waste on a troublemaker."

After my personal *thrilla*, I kept my head on a swivel in case someone else tried to sucker punch me. Larry and I now had bad-boy reputations, but honestly, we probably drew more spectators because of it. Our next battle, thankfully not a physical one, was with the league and the referees who cheated to make sure our Gilbey's Gin team didn't win games.

For example, Larry and I were the two best players in the league, hands-down. The sportswriters called us Gilbey's Villains. Believing they had to do something about this, the PBA officials changed the rules in the middle of the season so that no team could have two Americans on the court at the same time. Every time Larry was in the game, I had to come out, and vice versa. They didn't want the two of us dominating their local players anymore.

Our Gilbey's Gin team finished in third place that season. I averaged about 40 points a game, but I was still struggling to overcome the dark, ugly cloud that had been hanging over me since that first game—the fight, the crowd riot, the arrest, my new boss's understandable rage at me, my latest reputation as the "Villain of the PBA."

All things considered, you'd think I would have been yearning to get the hell out of there the minute I'd completed my contractual obligation to Honey Boy. But the truth was, I loved the Philippines. I felt like I was being paid to play basketball in paradise. Looking out at the ocean, and the mountains with picturesque rice paddies carved into them. The beautiful, exotic women. The Pacific lobsters and tiger shrimp and San Miguel beer. The hot days and cool nights. I'd lie on the beach and stare at the stars that went all the way to the horizon and, for the first time in longer than I can remember, feel as if maybe my life was going to turn out okay after all.

When the official Gilbey's Gin season ended, Ferdinand Marcos, president of the Philippines, brought in the current NBA champions, the Washington Bullets, to play an exhibition All-Star game in Manila. The Filipino team consisted of seven Americans and eight Filipino National Team members. The Bullets and their coach, Dick Motta, rolled into Manila with an incredible roster: Hall of Famers Wes Unseld and Elvin Hayes, Bobby Dandridge, Kevin Porter, George Trapp, Greg Ballard, and several other great players.

President Marcos was cheered by the huge crowd when he was introduced before the game began. I ended up scoring 22 points, and Larry McNeill scored 28, making him the highest scorer on both teams, but the Bullets won 111–100.

Much more memorable was that after the game, President Marcos invited us to a party at his palace, hosted by him and his wife Imelda.

Of course, the palace was unbelievable. It was surrounded by a moat and protected by armed military, a fierce-looking helicopter, and more security cameras than I'd ever seen in my life. Uniformed guards escorted us into the palace, where President and Imelda Marcos were entertaining their dozens of guests among the banana flowers, orchids, marble floors, and solid jade statues.

During the celebration, we were taken on a grand tour of the palace that included a scenic view of Imelda Marcos's famous collection of 5,000 pairs of shoes. After the tour, I even slow-danced with her, and I had a one-on-one conversation with President Marcos. We got along well until I asked him why there were so many people starving in the Philippines. Bad idea.

President Marcos pounded his fist on the table. "These people are ignorant and uneducated and need to be ruled with an iron fist. I know the Filipino Constitution and the United States Constitution backwards and forwards, and I know how to rule here in the Philippines."

I just nodded and made a note to myself not to ask this man any more questions. It was common knowledge that Marcos regularly sent his troops into the mountains to kill as many of his political rivals, who called themselves the New People's Army, as they could. What wasn't common knowledge was Marcos's fascination with Americans. I would have guessed that dictators would prefer the company of other dictators, but I would have guessed wrong—that man seemed to love being around us Americans at the party that night, even those of us who asked questions that offended him.

Before I left Manila, I did accidentally stumble into the dark side of Filipino politics. One night a few buddies and I went to a flashy, popular local disco. We were having a great time drinking, dancing, and just being boys, when all of a sudden the whole place was filled with tear gas. Unbeknownst to us until that moment, Marcos's son was at that same disco, and the New People's Army had launched the attack on the club.

I hadn't struggled to breathe through clouds of tear gas since military boot camp, and it's something I wouldn't wish on my worst enemy. Everyone else in the place was struggling as much as I was, and desperately stampeding toward the door. Being a very, very tall, strong athlete, I was able to push and shove my way out of there with the best of them, and I escaped with life and limb fully intact. So much for hanging out at Manila disco nightclubs.

I apparently hadn't quite had enough drama in the Philippines, because I also voluntarily dived into my first taste of entrepreneurship.

While I was playing for Gilbey's Gin and wanting to look as stylish off the court as I possibly could, I was introduced to a master tailor in Manila. His name was Lito Hogosohose, and he was so good at his craft that he could take your measurements, make a pattern on brown paper, cut the material from the pattern, sew it together, and have a perfect three-piece suit ready for fitting in eight hours. I'd never seen anything like it.

He and I spent a lot of time talking while he was making suits for me, and my heart went out to him—here he was, a good, hard-working man with lots of talent, and he'd never been out of the Philippines. He wanted more than anything to go to the United States and build a new and better life for himself and his family, but from the window of his cluttered little tailor shop, that dream looked about as realistic as hoping to land on the moon someday.

I happened to know a little something about having a dream, talent, and no money. I'd also been blessed that year, bumps in the road and all, thanks to a helping hand from my buddy Larry McNeill. Maybe it was time for me to reach out a helping hand to Lito, and not do myself any harm either. Maybe he and I could go into business together in Seattle—between his tailoring skills and my contacts, I couldn't imagine this not being profitable for both of us. The ecstatic disbelief on his face when I proposed the idea to him made it already feel like payback enough.

Between his visa and all the legal paperwork it took to get Lito out of the Philippines and into the United States, I'd already spent a lot of money, but it was going to be worth it to get this business up and running. Once we'd settled into my house in Seattle, I spent another $10,000 on the equipment he'd need—high-powered sewing machines, a serge machine, a buttonholer, hemming machines, electric scissors, you name it. We set up his shop in the basement, where there was plenty of room, and we were off and running.

Two months later, we landed a contract with Alaska Airlines to sew all their flight attendant uniforms and aprons. Then came a flurry of suit orders for NBA players, at $800–$1,000 per tailor-made suit. We even made a few suits for Bill Russell. I'd already seen what a hard worker Lito was, and I was always out soliciting customers, so he and I rarely saw each other. I was feeling really good about the possibility of a steady income that had nothing to do with the whims and personalities of coaches and basketball leagues, and I was sure Lito was feeling exactly the same way.

Several weeks later I bounded out of bed one morning with a full day of potential client calls ahead of me. I headed to the basement to greet Lito and was surprised to find that he wasn't there—he'd always started work by the time I woke up, but oh, well, maybe the poor guy had slept in for a change. He deserved it. He'd been working his ass off on the Alaska Airlines commitment, so he had to have been exhausted.

I walked around the house. It was oddly silent, and still no Lito. It wasn't until I went into his bedroom that my heart sank. The closet doors were standing open, and all his clothes were gone.

I couldn't believe it. What the hell had happened? What went wrong? Why hadn't he talked to me about whatever it was? Where had he gone? Would he be back? And what was I supposed to do now . . . ?

I was going crazy asking myself all those questions I couldn't possibly answer when the phone rang. Yes! It had to be Lito, right?

Wrong. It was my old buddy and Seattle teammate Slick Watts. But what do you know, *he* had answers. Crazy ones, but at least now I knew.

There was a guy named Boris who was a rep for a Maryland company named Bata that made sneakers for NBA teams. They'd started with Bata Bullets for the Washington Bullets that became so popular the company expanded to other teams, and Boris had ended up making sneaker deals and becoming friends with some of the Sonics players, including Slick and me.

So Boris told Slick, who told me on the phone that day, that he and Lito had gotten acquainted, and Lito had begun confiding in him. It seems that Lito was desperately missing his family, his country, and his native food, but he was afraid to ask me for help getting back to the Philippines because I'd already invested so much money in him and our tailoring business.

To avoid having to confront me, Lito decided to leave me, the United States, and everything else behind while I was sleeping, and it was Boris who helped make it all happen. To hell with the cash I'd laid out getting Lito to Seattle, or the $10,000 worth of tailoring equipment I'd bought that was now sitting there useless in my basement, or the unfulfilled contracts with Alaska Airlines and some other clients I'd have to reimburse. And, obviously, to hell with what had started to become a profitable business, and to hell with me.

Well, the feeling was mutual, that's for sure. I felt completely betrayed, emotionally and financially. So to hell with my friendships with Lito, and Boris, too. I was broke. Again. With no foreseeable income in my future. Again.

It was time for the International Basketball Vagabond Bandit to turn to the only thing I knew I was good at, that had kept bailing me out for all these years. I was pretty sure Honey Boy wouldn't exactly welcome back the Villain of the PBA with open arms, but if I looked hard enough and spread the word far enough, someone would. And I was right.

Next stop: South America.

Chapter Thirteen

I managed to find a gig that was roughly comparable to my contract in the Philippines, in Valencia, Venezuela, playing for a team called Trotamundos de Carabobo. One of the first people I met was another American player named Larry Spicer, who would become one of my teammates, my apartment roommate, and one of my best friends for life. Larry had played college basketball at Baylor before getting drafted by the Milwaukee Bucks. We were both Black and 6-feet-9-inches tall, and boy, did we stand out in Venezuela, but the people there were great to us.

Larry and I had had our share of nicknames throughout our basketball careers. I was "Tree" in Arkansas. Twiggy in Seattle. Deano in the Philippines. In Valencia, I became *Jirafa* (giraffe). To Larry McNeill and Larry Spicer, I was Dean the Dream, which I always liked—my life, after all, had been one long, uninterrupted dream, sometimes amazing beyond belief and sometimes nothing short of a nightmare. I immediately dubbed Larry "the Ice Machine," because he was so smooth and cool.

Larry/Ice was homesick when I got there, and he'd been thinking about going back to his hometown of Memphis, Tennessee. He had two complaints about Valencia: "I can't get a decent haircut, and I can't stomach the food, so I have to cook all my own meals."

So Larry gave me yet another nickname when we moved into our apartment—"Godsend"—when he found out that I knew my way around a kitchen thanks to all the years I'd spent cooking for my brothers and sister. I'd also brought my waffle iron with me, and, as a veteran, I got great prices on American groceries on the local military base. I couldn't help Larry with the haircut thing, but when eating wasn't a problem

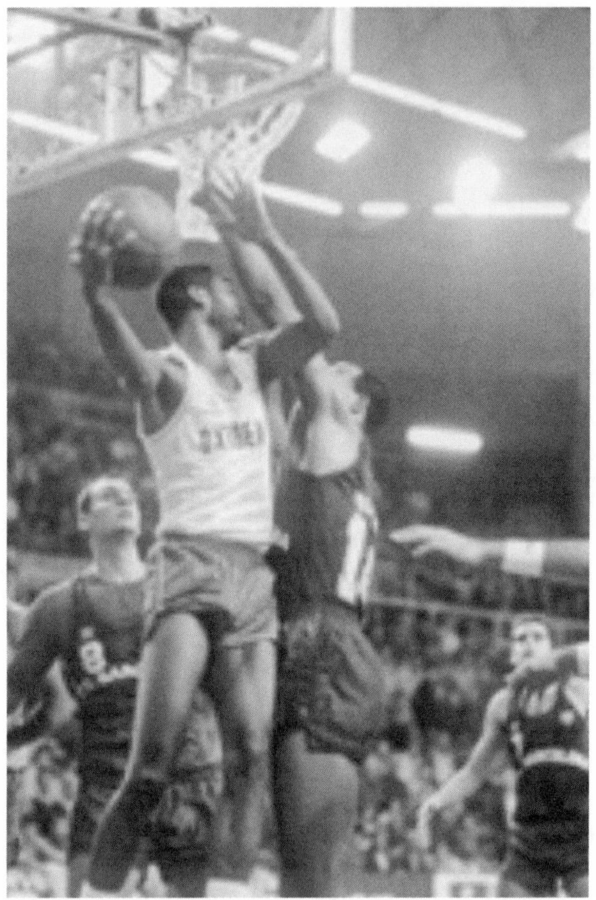

International teammate Larry Spicer
COURTESY OF THE AUTHOR

anymore, he decided that maybe he wasn't really as homesick for Tennessee as he'd thought he was.

We went to a few days of basketball practice to meet our coach, Pedro Espinoza, and get into the swing of things. Then we won our first game. I scored 30 points and grabbed 20 rebounds. Spicer scored 31 points.

I had to give him a little bit of a hard time about it. "Hey, Ice, how in the hell did you outscore me?"

"Dream, what do you think I'm doing here in Venezuela? I'm not on vacation!" he told me. "There's a clause in our contracts that says if we go all the way to the championship, we get an extra five grand. If you think I can't use an extra five grand, you're crazy, man."

Since I still couldn't read, I'd missed that fine print when I signed my contract. An extra five grand on top of our salary sounded damned good to me too.

"You're right, let's get busy, Spicer."

And we did. We played hard, we practiced hard, and we jogged for hours every day on the beautiful white sands of the beaches to stay in shape. We were looking good, our team was looking good, and life was looking good . . . for the most part.

I don't know about now, but back then, to play basketball in Venezuela, you had to love the game, because nothing came easily. Six-hour bus trips were the norm. One time we had a game up in the Andes mountains. The bus drove along the side of a mountain on a road so narrow, Larry and I saw our lives flash before our eyes. There were white crosses all along the side of the road where people had accidentally driven off the cliffs and died. As we drove farther and farther up into the clouds, we realized that our lives were in the hands of the stranger behind the wheel who might be a suicidal maniac for all we knew. We were so terrified that we insisted on flying back to Valencia from that game.

But hey, if you could survive life-threatening bus rides, watching locals slaughter animals on the side of the road to feed their families, and having to pick your food carefully enough so you didn't get dysentery, you might live long enough to get paid. It wasn't easy. Every time payday came along, we dealt with all kinds of problems and excuses.

South America had a bad rap when it came to paying its players, so the International Vagabond Bandito set the rules right up front. This was my money we were talking about. I only knew three or four words in Spanish, but I knew how to make myself understood. And who was going to argue with an angry giraffe?

I quickly developed the Dean Tolson strategy, which worked like this: When I got off the plane, there'd be a guy to pick me up, holding a "Dean Tolson" sign. I'd say, "Hello, I'm Dean." The man with the sign would nod and say, "*Vamos al gymnasio a practicar pronto.*"

"No, *amigo*," I would reply, "we go *pronto* to *El Banco, por favor.*"

"*El Banco*?"

I'd explain, as simply and firmly as possible, before we'd even left the airport, that I wasn't going to the *gymnasio* or anywhere else until I got paid in full for the coming month. If the answer was no, then I'd make a show of turning around and heading back toward the plane. It never failed.

During that season, I slipped on a court that was wet from a leaky arena roof and hurt my knee so badly that I wanted to go home. It turns out that I tore my right ACL, and there wasn't a magical surgery in those days to fix ACL tears. I'm sure I would have flown straight back to the United States if it hadn't been for Larry—I couldn't leave him there by himself, so I stayed and played on that bad knee.

We played well and ended the season in the playoffs, eventually coming in second. The owner of the team still owed Larry and me around $10,000 each, so we went to Coach Espinoza's office and asked, "Where's the owner?"

He shrugged. "Haven't seen him since the Wykria game."

He had nothing more to say, and neither did we, so we headed to a small nearby bodega to conspire over coffee.

"When I first came to town," I said, "the owner took me to his house, so I know where it is. What do you say we head over there, hang out under a bush and wait for him, and then nab him first chance we get?"

With $10,000 on the line that he was rightfully owed, Larry was all for it.

So that night, Larry and I were hiding under the thick pink bougainvillea by the owner's front door, ready to pounce.

I whispered, "When he opens the door to go in, I'll jump out, push him into the house, and sit on him. You follow us in, shut the door behind us, and we'll have him. Just remember, we gotta do this right, or we could get in a whole hell of a lot of trouble."

Larry looked at me, visibly nervous about this. I wasn't exactly thrilled either that we'd been reduced to strong-arming a guy just to collect our salary, but we were where we were.

"I've done this before. It works," I reassured him. "The season's over, and this guy thinks we're on a plane back to the States right now. He's not counting on coming face-to-face with the Vagabond Bandit and his sidekick, the Iceman."

Moments later, the team owner got home, arrived at his front door, unlocked it, and stepped inside, leaving the door open just long enough for me to jump out of the bushes, tackle him to the floor, and sit on him. Spicer sprang in like a cat and closed the front door behind him.

The owner was squealing, "*Por favor, amigo*, release, release! Or I call *policia*!"

I picked his butt off the floor and pinned him to the wall. "Where's the *dinero, señor*?"

The little man kicked like a kid, his heels pounding against the wall.

"Listen, Chinga," I growled at him, "you're gonna cough up our *dinero, muy pronto*! *Comprende*?"

Larry yelled at me to put him down. I admit it, I was enjoying the fear on that cowardly crook's face, which I pointed out to Larry with a smile. "Look at him, Ice. He's already saying goodbye to that money."

I let the owner slide down the wall like a slug, still holding him by his collar. Then I released him but stayed close enough that he could feel my breath while I smoothed his twisted collar, straightened his necktie, and patted out the wrinkles in his suitcoat.

"Give us our *dinero*. Our due and payable. Now!"

"*Uno momento*," the little son of a bitch croaked out. He nodded toward the bedroom, and we followed him and watched him pull a metal money box out from under the bed. It hit us later how crazy we were to do that—he could have pulled a gun out of that box and shot us both. Two enormous Black guys in his house, standing over him in his bedroom? He would have kept his money and not even been arrested.

But in our defense, when he opened the box, we saw nothing but American $100 bills. He sat on the tile floor and counted out $10,000 for me and the same for Spicer.

Only one thing left on the to-do list: Get the hell out of Dodge!

We floored it to our condo, packed up, and shipped out fast. Taxi to Caracas. Hotfoot it to the airport gate. On the plane. Gone.

This is why, whenever a player joins a team in a foreign country, they should remember the cardinal rules: Don't leave the States without a contract, a round-trip plane ticket, and a passport. Always get paid when you get off the plane. And make sure you get your final payment as you walk off the court.

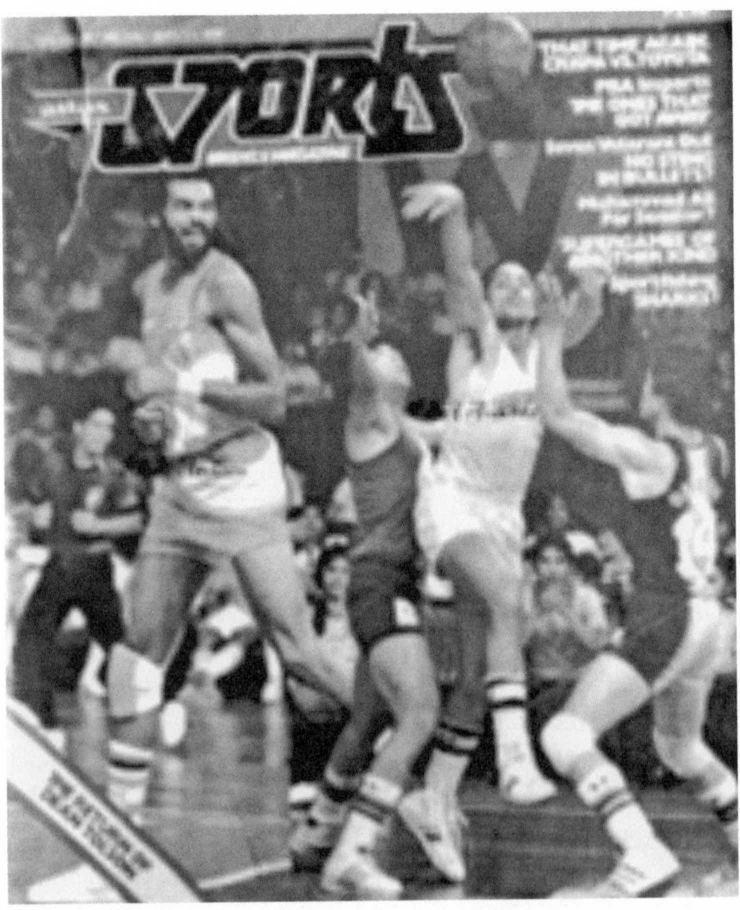

Philippines International League action
COURTESY OF THE AUTHOR

So there I was, back in Seattle, unemployed again. There was getting to be a certain sameness to this . . . no job, no money coming in to cover my bills, and then, thank God, sooner or later, the phone rings . . .

This call caught me completely off guard. It was from Adolpho Ferrier, Honey Boy's CPA in the Philippines.

"Deano, how about another season in Manila?"

Surprised as I was, I cut right to the chase. "Are we talking about the same money as before?"

"Same money, Deano."

What do you know—the Villain of the PBA was being invited back to the Philippines as good old Deano, everybody's pal.

And good old Deano was no fool. I was on a plane the next day, ready to work hard, play hard, and win again for Honey Boy to make up for what I'd put him through last time around.

But first, I had some unfinished business to take care of.

I went straight to Luzon Provence, outside Manila.

Lito's neighborhood.

There were kids playing in the street. I must have looked like Goliath to them when I loomed toward them, but they all smiled when they saw me, and I smiled back to make sure they knew I wouldn't hurt them for anything in the world. I asked if they knew where Lito Hogosohose lived, and they pointed to a mud hut with a grass roof.

A girl I assumed was Lito's daughter answered the door when I knocked. I could see past her to a chicken running around on the dirt floor.

"Papa, it's for you," she called out.

Lito appeared, and burst into tears when he saw me.

"Deano, I'm sorry, I'm so sorry, Deano," he said, sobbing, before he fell to his knees and started massaging my feet.

Oh, please. "Don't be doing that, Lito. Get up."

He awkwardly got to his feet. I stared at him, shaking my head as it hit me all over again how much he'd hurt me. "Man, all you had to do is come to me. We could have worked it out. I thought we were friends. You didn't have to run out on me like that."

His eyes were wet, and I thought he might fall apart again. His voice was trembling when he finally spoke. "How can I repay you?"

I gestured around his tiny mud shack. "Obviously, you can't."

"Please, Deano," he pleaded, "you need to understand. I missed my family so bad. I missed my kids so much. I just couldn't bear it. I was dying in America. Let me do something to make it up to you, maybe make some free clothes for you . . ."

I was done with this conversation. "Okay, fine," I said. "Make me some clothes. But remember this—I gave you the opportunity of a lifetime, Lito, and you disappeared on me without even saying goodbye. No one will ever do something like that for you again. Do you get that?"

He nodded slowly, and I walked away. I didn't know or care if I'd ever get those free clothes. That was laughably beside the point. I'd said what I had to say, I was done, I could put Lito behind me once and for all, and it felt good.

The Gilbey's Gin season started, and with every game we played, my ACL injury got worse. And any time a game got physical, they threatened to deport me.

I finished the season, but I was over it. I flew home and never played in the Philippines again.

The next season, 1982–83, I returned to Valencia and the Carabobo team. Larry Spicer had signed on with another team in Venezuela, so I had two new American teammates—Winfred Bowen from the LA Lakers, and Sylvester Cuyler from the Lancaster Red Roses.

They found out I was making more money than they were, and they resented the hell out of me for it. We argued a lot, which doesn't make for a successful basketball team.

"If you're not happy with what you're being paid, tell it to the owner, not to me. I'm out of this," I repeatedly yelled at them. And I meant it in more ways than one—when the season ended, so did my basketball career in South America . . . until next time.

I flew straight to Seattle from Venezuela and acted on a decision I'd been considering for a long time—I put my house up for sale, and moved my aunt in and my girlfriend out. I wanted to get rid of that house ASAP. I made a deal with my aunt that I'd wire her money to pay the bills and the mortgage, and she'd put anything left over in the bank for me so I'd always have money when I returned. In exchange, she'd live in my house rent-free and just pay the utilities. When I got back home from my next gig, I found out she'd been saving all the extra money to buy a condo and a car for herself. I was running out of people to trust.

That "next gig" was in 1983, when I flew to Amsterdam to link up with my good friend Rudy Jackson, a 6'10" center from New York City. Rudy had married a Dutch woman, which allowed him to stay in Holland and not have to travel all over the place.

I stayed with Rudy for three months in search of a basketball contract in Europe. The two of us spent a lot of time on the phone with a translator, wrangling contracts, and when we weren't on the phone, we were usually jogging around Amsterdam to stay in shape.

One day on a jog, Rudy looked at my right knee and did a double-take. "What happened there, man?" he asked.

I told him about tearing my ACL on a wet court during that game in Venezuela.

He sympathized. "I did the same thing. No wonder both of our legs look goofy. We're the crooked-leg twins, right?!"

"Hurts like hell," I added. "Yours too, huh?"

"It did, until I got hooked up with this chiropractor in town who helped me a lot. I'll take you over there."

Yet another bonus in the life of an international basketball player—a guy knows a guy who knows a guy who knows a doctor. So off we went.

Four people worked me over on a long table, said my whole spinal cord was out of alignment, and gave me an adjustment. One visit and I felt better. Two, and I felt almost right. Sold. I ended up going to them for the entire three months I was in Amsterdam. Their most common treatment, which they did over and over again, was to put my body on a traction table, lift me by my skin, and drop my whole body back down on the table.

It sounds like torture. But no, torture was walking on a bum knee and having back pain every day of my life. After Rudy's chiropractor pummeling me every week for three months, there was no doubt about it, I had a better range of motion in my leg and was able to keep playing pretty damned well on that damaged knee.

After staying with Rudy and his wife in Amsterdam for 90 days that summer, I had to leave. A Dutch law dictates that if you stay in the country for longer than 90 days, you become a public charge of the Dutch government.

By then, Larry McNeill was playing in the Canary Islands in Spain, and he got word to me that he could help me find some exhibition games in Europe.

I'd been on exhibition tours when I first got cut from the Sonics. You play in these games, and European scouts who like you will try to sign you. Back in 1975, an Italian team owner offered me a $100,000 contract to play for his team. I was so sure I'd be signing with another NBA team that I turned him down, and he was so infuriated that he flipped a whole dining table at me, spaghetti and all.

But times definitely change, don't they? I wanted a job, I needed a job, and thanks again to my great friend Larry McNeill, I got a job, on the exhibition circuit.

Before long I was approached by a guy named Nikko Belbus, who was a spectator at one of the games in Spain. Nikko drove a tourist bus for a big outfit in Athens, Greece, and he couldn't have been more enthusiastic when he shook my hand after the game.

"You're a fantastic player," he told me. "Why don't I just take you to Greece now and find you a basketball job?"

He seemed like a nice man, I'd never seen Greece, I had nothing to lose, and I sure as hell knew I could take care of myself if this turned out badly, so . . .

"Okay," I said, "sounds good."

And off I went to Greece on a bus with Nikko and his tourist passengers. I didn't exactly blend in with the other tourists, and they kept gawking at me, probably assuming Nikko had hired this Black colossus as a security guard or something. They were all speaking Greek, of course, so I couldn't understand a word anyone said, but it was one of the most spectacular bus rides of my life. The rolling countryside from Spain to Greece was home to castles, farms, gentle hills and valleys, and plains of green that stretched on forever. It was the experience of a lifetime, one of those rare places that make your heart ache like homesickness, even though you've never been there before.

A day later, in Athens, Nikko restored a little of my faith in humanity when he kept his word and took me to meet four basketball teams: Panathinaikos, Olympia Coast, Sparta, and A.E.K. (pronounced "Ike"). All four teams were sponsored by large import/export ocean liner firms with a lot of money. And I do mean "a lot of money"—for example, Aristotle Onassis's company Olympic Maritime was one of the team owners.

Nikko hooked me up with A.E.K., one of the oldest teams in Greece. If I remember correctly, Kurt Rambis played with A.E.K. before he went on to play for the Los Angeles Lakers.

Greek team starting five
COURTESY OF THE AUTHOR

I happily signed a contract to play for $30,000 a season. Because of an odd rule, Americans could only play in Europe Cup games, not in local games within the country. That meant I was on a Greek team but wasn't allowed to play a single game in Greece. So I'd practice every day with the team, but when they played a game in their home country, I didn't suit up. Instead, I'd pass the days sightseeing and taking photos with my trusty Canon A-E1.

It was such a nice life. I lived in the La Fattah Hotel on the beach. Nikko always went to the local games and came by to check on me, and he routinely took me all over Athens to some of its finest restaurants.

I played my first game for A.E.K. against Luxembourg in the Europe Cup. I scored 40 points, and we won easily. I was warned, though, that as we moved forward in the Cup, the games would get harder. Next, we played and won against the German team, but it was definitely a tougher game. Then came games against Italy and France. Rumor had it that their teams were good, so we practiced hard back in Athens for another week to prepare.

One night after a long road trip, I fell asleep as soon as my body made contact with the bed. I'm not sure how much time passed before I was awakened by a weird sensation of some kind of lateral movement. I opened my eyes to discover that my bed was sliding from one side of the room to the other like some bizarre paranormal amusement park ride. It seemed to go on and on before it stopped as suddenly as it had started. Later that day at practice, one of my Greek teammates asked if I'd felt the strong earthquake the night before.

"An earthquake? I remember my bed sliding around, but I thought I was dreaming," I said.

"Well, that was an earthquake," he replied, and everyone laughed at me for going through my first earthquake and not having a clue what it was.

Dean Smith and Michael Jordan showed up in Athens that year with the University of North Carolina Tar Heels for an exhibition game. My knee was killing me, so they made me sit out that game. It was Michael's sophomore year, the season after he hit the game-winning shot against Georgetown to win the NCAA Championship. At that game in Athens,

Michael Jordan was just another exceptional college athlete. Strange to look back and realize that this legendary superstar had once been a kid on his way up.

Shortly after we left for our game in France, the pain in my knee had intensified so much that I could hardly run up and down the floor. The French team had a center who was a naturalized African, a guy no less than 7-feet-2 and about 375 pounds, and he looked mean and ugly. For the first and only time in my career, I was facing a player I feared.

I only scored 11 points that night. Sadly, this loss eliminated our team from the Europe Cup, but with my sore knee and a giant at my heels, I couldn't even get close to the basket.

With that, my season in Greece ended, and my knee was screaming at me to get an operation. To make matters worse, I had trouble getting my final pay from the Greek owner of the team. But this time, no bushwhacking was required. I caught up with him at a soccer game, and that's when he asked if I'd come back to Greece to play the following season. That was a quick, easy "yes!"

I wrapped up my business in Greece. At the top of the priority list was thanking Nikko Belbus for . . . everything. His kindness. His generosity. His friendship. The undeniable fact that if it hadn't been for him, I would never have had the pleasure of playing basketball in his wonderful country. He was gracious as always when we said goodbye, and I can still see his smile when I told him I'd be back in a few months.

I had no idea that wasn't true, that I would never see Nikko or Greece again.

Chapter Fourteen

"You look horrible, son!"

That's how Mother greeted me when I flew from Athens to Kansas City to visit her for the summer.

"I haven't heard from you in almost four years. You running all over playing your basketball, making money, having fun seeing the world, and you really don't care about nothing, not even your own self. And you come in here like some hotshot, basketball under your arm, all that money you made overseas gone, and you living out of a suitcase!"

I knew I was going to get an earful from her when I got home. It was one thing when I was playing basketball in the United States. A flight to Kansas City was no big deal. But I'd been all over the globe in the past four years, so a quick trip to see my mother wasn't exactly practical. And those four years were starting to take a toll. The pain in my knee was worse than ever, and I knew I wasn't the same player I used to be. I'd learned to adapt my game so I could keep scoring. I could still spin past guys and lay the ball into the basket, and I was playing at a high enough level to keep getting paid. But I wasn't dunking from all over the court anymore. I wasn't a force to be reckoned with, or the guy other teams had to strategize against, and having to admit that to myself was almost more painful than my damned knee.

Mother let out a sigh, gave me a long, disappointed look, and tore into me some more. I sat there like a soldier and took it, because Mother was always right, even when she was wrong. No matter what, I always listened to her.

"You're 32 years old, son. How much longer you think you can keep playing basketball?"

Mother barbecueing
COURTESY OF AUTHOR

I shrugged. I'd always avoided asking myself that question, and I didn't want to hear it.

"You're not a young man anymore, and you don't have no education. What's gonna happen if you break a leg out there, or hurt your back? You'll have nothing, that's what. You've been playing basketball all this time, but when are you gonna *do something* with your life?"

That one cut me to the bone. I thought living my dream *was* doing something with my life. I wanted to play NBA ball, and I did it. When that dream was taken away from me, I kept going. I made good money playing overseas. I'd been to places I'd never imagined seeing, and I didn't even have to wear an Army uniform to do it. I was having fun. Wasn't that *something*?

I waited until she took a breath, and then I squeaked, "Mother, I'm happy with my life. I've been doing what I wanted to do since I was nine years old—playing basketball . . ."

"Stop it! You're being foolish, Dean!" she interrupted. "That's not gonna last forever." She cocked her head to one side and aimed a cocked eyebrow at me. "You think you're gonna be playing basket when you're 50? Is that what you think? You can't be that crazy."

I looked away from her, trying to come up with a good defense. There wasn't one, until she added, "You need to go back to college and get you some sort of an education. The way you like to make money and spend money, you better get something going for yourself before it's too late."

Okay, finally she'd lobbed something to me I could actually work with.

"Mother, think about it. I'm illiterate! We both know that! Why would you even ask me to go back to college and try to graduate at my age?"

I thought we were just having a typical mother-son debate. It caught me completely off-guard when she started to cry.

"Honey, your daddy and I only got to the eighth grade, and you . . . you're smarter than that."

She dabbed her eyes with a napkin but kept on crying as she went on in a soft voice. "Truth is, no one in the history of this family ever graduated. Not your Uncle Raymond, your Uncle Tiken, your Uncle Ralph, your Uncle Eugene, your Aunt Bonnie . . . you even got a basketball scholarship, you had your education paid for, and you didn't take advantage of it. All you did was play ball." Then she looked right at me and added, "It would mean the world to me to see you graduate from college one day."

This conversation was hitting way too close to home, and I needed to end it. So I straightened my shoulders and informed her, "Mother, I just got back from Athens, Greece. One of the most beautiful places I've ever seen. I got offered a contract to play basketball there again, I'm going to do it, and that's the way it is."

She didn't say a word, she just shuffled away into the kitchen and started making supper. In fact, she barely said a word to me for the next two weeks. I was like a ghost wandering around in her house. She'd walk right past me as if I wasn't even there, and if I asked her a question, she'd just silently shrug and keep on going. She may have been silent, but the message was loud and clear: She was painfully disappointed in me for not recognizing that, as far as she was concerned, I was headed nowhere.

I fumbled around the house like an unwanted guest with nowhere to go until I was just a few days away from my flight back to Greece. That's when I noticed that my plane ticket, passport, and contract were missing.

I asked Mother if she'd seen them.

"No," she said. She lied so rarely that she was really terrible at it.

"I laid them right here on top of my bedroom dresser, and that's where they should be. Seeing as how there's just the two of us in the house . . . well, I know one thing for sure—they didn't hop down from the dresser and go running off by themselves."

She took that in, and believe me, there was no apology in her voice when she spoke up.

"Yes," she said, "I saw them. But you ain't gettin' 'em back unless you go down there to Arkansas and enroll in that college, go back to school, and try to graduate."

"Mother, you're crazy! Give me my stuff!"

She took her sweet time. She knew I was angry, so maybe she was giving me time to cool down. Or maybe I inherited my stubbornness from her, as if I hadn't figured that out years ago. But when she got good and ready, she went up to the attic. I heard her rummaging around up there, and then she came back downstairs with my plane ticket, passport, and contract in her hand. Instead of handing them over, she said, "Sit down, son. Let's talk."

It's funny how the smallest details of moments like this stay with you, but I remember clear as a bell that when we pulled up our chairs to the kitchen table, these great big raindrops started pelting the kitchen window and running down it like tears.

"I know you can't read or write," she began, "but let me ask you something I should have asked a long, long time ago, and I want the truth: Have you ever *tried* to learn to read and write?"

I thought of a million things I could say. No, I never tried, because no one ever cared if I could read or write. Teachers, students, coaches, teammates . . . they didn't care, they never wanted to know the real Dean Tolson. They cheated to get me in school, and they cheated to get me out. The only Dean Tolson they wanted to know was the one who could take off from behind the free throw line and dunk a basketball. That's how the system does you. Once you move on to the next level, you're someone else's problem. I made my own way without anyone even asking about my literacy, or my GPA, for that matter, and when I played international leagues and sold my talent to the highest bidder, it didn't even matter if I could read or write English. As long as fans were in the seats and team owners were happy, I was welcome, illiterate or not.

Rather than laying all that out, though, I left it at a simple, "Honestly, Mother, no, I haven't tried."

"Well, you know, I've never asked you kids to do nothing for me, but now, I'm asking you. Please. Do this for me." She was crying again, and it was raining harder. "Dean, if you're going to keep playing ball, you will break my heart."

I believed her, I was just a little incredulous to hear her put it so plainly. "It really means more than anything to you that I go back to school and graduate?"

She nodded, and then handed me my plane ticket, my passport, and my contract to play the next season in Greece. "I love you, son, and I hope you make the right decision. In fact, if you'll go back to school, I'll give you $50 every month to help you out."

I chuckled. "$50 a month? Mother, I make $5,000 a month playing ball."

"That's all I can afford," she said quietly, and it tore me up. She loved me so much, and wanted the best for me so much, that she was willing to give me what little extra she had every month to prove it.

So right then and there, at 32 years of age, I made the decision to retire from basketball, go back to school, and prove to my mother, and myself, that I could overcome my illiteracy if, for the first time in my life, I really tried. Besides, let's face it, if I was sitting in a classroom, what difference would it make that my right knee was shot to hell?

I truly loved the game. I never even got married, because a wife would have always come in second, and that wouldn't have been fair to anyone. The only person on this earth I could imagine loving more than I loved basketball was my mother, and if I had to give one of them up, it wasn't going to be her.

So I made the last call I wanted to make—I dialed Frank Broyles, former head football coach of the Arkansas Razorbacks for 18 years. He won an NCAA Championship with the Razorbacks, which made him a deity in Arkansas. The same year I left the university for the NBA, Frank became the school's athletic director, which made him the most powerful and highest-paid man in the state. Frank Broyles was the voice of God at the University of Arkansas.

"Hey, Coach, it's Tree. How are you?"

You would have thought we'd just talked the day before. "I'm fine, Tree. What can I do for you?"

"Well, my mother wants me to go back to school and get my degree. What do you think about that?"

"Are you kidding? I think that's just wonderful! When would you like to get started?"

"Right now, Coach."

"Then get on down here, Tree, and let's get you enrolled."

It felt like divine intervention. First my mother begged me to stop wasting time playing ball and finally, legitimately, graduate from college. Then Coach Broyles backed her up by being so positive, and so easy with me after such a long time. I was fresh out of arguments. Apparently this was a great idea . . .

Except that I didn't have a car.

But more divine intervention. It was actually getting a little spooky. My brother Brent just happened to have *two* cars, one of which was a green 1973 Pontiac Grand Prix. "Dean, you can have it if you want it," he said as I was looking it over. "It ain't all that good-lookin,' but it's transportation."

As far as I was concerned, "free" more than made up for "not that good-lookin.'" I threw some clothes in a bag, kissed my very happy mother goodbye, took that car, and hit the road, off to see Coach Frank Broyles and, I hoped, enroll at the University of Arkansas. Again.

I was very surprised when I got to Fayetteville. I'd been gone for less than 10 years, but the campus looked totally different. The football stadium that used to hold 59,000 people could now hold 82,000, and it had a $100 million plasma instant replay screen. Next on my personal Coach Frank Broyles tour: the new 23,000-seat Bud Walton Basketball Arena.

During the tour, Coach Broyles told me about his own journey over the past decade. He'd become a born-again Christian, and he'd made and kept a vow to lay his racism down at the altar in order to be a better man. And now, as the athletic director, he'd also become determined to make education a priority for student-athletes at the University of Arkansas and see more athletes graduate every year.

"If you'd come to me 10 years ago, Tree, I probably wouldn't have helped you," he told me. "But we failed you the first time, so we owe you the opportunity to graduate. So now that our little campus tour is over, let's get you enrolled . . . if you're willing to give me a total commitment."

"No problem, Coach. Do you need me to sign something?"

"No, just a handshake and a promise you won't be skipping classes and goofing off like you did last time."

I was embarrassed. He was exactly right, I did squander the first opportunity I'd had to get a first-rate college education. I sheepishly shook his hand, but I lowered my head and stared at my feet while I did it. "I promise you, I'm going to be a real student this time."

"I need a handshake and an eyeball from you, Tree."

"Sorry." I raised my head and looked him in the eyes. "Coach, I will do everything in my power to graduate from the University of Arkansas."

"I'll hold you to that," he said with a smile. "Now, let's go to the administration building and get you enrolled."

Coach stood there with me in the office while an administrative assistant pulled up my old transcript: 40 hours of Ds and 40 hours of Fs. But in 1984, 10 years later, the university calculated grades differently. My 40 hours of Ds turned into another 40 hours of Fs. That meant that from 1970 to 1974, I accumulated a total of 80 hours of Fs on a 124-hour transcript. They declared me incapable of doing the work and refused to enroll me.

The registrar, a formally dressed middle-aged woman, asked Coach Broyles the obvious question: "Why waste your time and the school's money trying to graduate this man?"

He was as firm as he was polite. "Because we owe it to him. If he's willing to do the work, we need to give him the opportunity."

As if I wasn't even standing there, she pointed out to him, "He'll have to make up 89 hours of course study in every class in which he got a D or an F. In essence, he'll have to repeat the entire four years if he wants to graduate."

Oh, God. I really hated to interrupt, but I had no choice. "Wait, are you saying that I have to pull my GPA from a 1.43 to a 2.0 in four years? Is that even possible? Has anyone ever done that before?"

The registrar shook her head. "No, because anyone with a 1.43 grade point average would have been dismissed from the university. You'd be better off going to another college and starting over. Trying to graduate from the University of Arkansas is a waste of time for you."

In other words, letting me declare academic bankruptcy and start over in Fayetteville was out of the question. If I was going to do this in Arkansas, I was going to have to crawl out of the hole I created, even though the university had never done this before. Otherwise, I'd be letting down Mother, Coach Broyles, and myself.

It was my turn to shake my head. "No, ma'am, I made this mess here at the University of Arkansas, and this is where I'm going to clean it up, if you'll just give me a chance."

After a fairly lengthy silence and a long look at me, she said, "I'll see what I can do."

And what do you know, she made it happen. Thanks to Frank Broyles and the Razorbacks Athletic Scholarship Fund, I was officially an illiterate student on a scholarship at the University of Arkansas, for the second time in my life.

Chapter Fifteen

So there I was again, trying to graduate college without knowing how to read or write. At this point, it seemed like even more of a moonshot than making it to the NBA. The look on that registrar's face in the admissions office said as much. But this time around, particularly with a lot of hard-won experience under my belt, good and bad, it felt different.

I was talented enough to make it to the NBA, but I'd had no way of knowing how many obstacles would be in the way once I got there. Guys making big money with guaranteed contracts standing in line ahead of me. An NBA legend for a coach who could do whatever he wanted and play the exact opposite style of play that I was suited for, and that the league was adapting to. The unspoken racial quotas that kept Black players like me from earning a spot on the end of a bench and the opportunity to prove themselves.

Now, as I started school again in 1984, I realized it was all on me. If I could learn to read and write and get some As, I would graduate. It brought out the competitive spirit in me. I was fueled by the rage I still felt about how I was treated in the NBA. I had made it to the pinnacle of professional sports, and those people still looked at me as a failure. I'd be damned if I'd ever be dismissed in that condescending way again, especially not by the likes of a Bill Russell. With no politics and biases to deal with, I might actually win this game all by myself.

There's an old saying that "when you do what you did, you get what you got." I wasn't about to do what I did—this time, I'd go in with a game plan. I started by making six vows to myself while I kept my *attention* and, most important, my *intention*, alive. If my intention stayed at the top of my priority list, how could I fail? Well, only if I let myself forget my six vows:

1. Never, ever skip a class for any reason.
2. Study and read my assigned chapters every night.
3. Sit front-row-center in every class.
4. Take all tests with my classmates; no make-ups.
5. Get to know each instructor personally.
6. Not leave the University of Arkansas until I graduate.

My agreement with Coach Broyles was to carry at least a 2.0 GPA each semester, and that first semester was brutal. It was sink or swim for me in the deep end of the academic pool. But thanks to those vows, even just showing up for class and sitting in the front row was a small daily victory.

Thanks to Study Skills 101, I began to learn how to read and study. It's almost as hard to explain how I finally learned to read as it was to actually learn how to read. I was the slowest student in the class, but I was also the most determined and the most competitive, so no way was I going to let this illiteracy thing beat me anymore, even though it was a very long, painful process. By then, I'd already pieced together a few basics—the letters of the alphabet, for example, and what each of them sounds like. Then, slowly but surely, I started being able to combine the letters and sounds into words on paper, and eventually break down words with more than one syllable and pronounce them, whether I knew what they meant or not. The definition part came later, as I went along.

When I was alone and studying, if there was a word I didn't understand, I would write it, erase it, write it again, erase it again . . . sometimes I would do that up to 500 times a day until I had the word memorized, even if it took me 15 hours a day—as it occasionally did.

I also got very good very quickly at blocking out distractions. I was a 32-year-old man in a dorm with 18-year-old kids who were away from home for the first time, which meant loud, nonstop partying. Well, been there, done that, and look where it got me. Even if I'd been tempted to "stop by," it just wasn't an option anymore. Instead, I made myself block out the noise and replaced it by developing a habit that worked for me: I'd get back to my dorm room and lay all my books from that day on my bed. Then I'd take one book at a time, tackle that assignment, put that book on the floor when the assignment was done, and move on to the next book and the next assignment. I didn't allow myself to go to sleep until all the books were off the bed. Some nights that meant 3:00 or 4:00 a.m. Some nights that meant no sleep at all.

But that Study Skills 101 course got me started on the right track, and it worked, because I made it work. I *let* it work, after fighting it since my first day of that stupid inconvenience called "school" when I was five or six years old. By the end of the course I even knew how to dissect a textbook, to skim, scan, and speed-read, and how to break a book down into its component parts. My grades for my first semester in 1984 were:

Study Skills 101 - A

US and World History, 1877 to Present - C

Foundation of Physical Education 1 - B

Special Population for the Handicapped - B

My GPA rounded out at 3.0. I wasn't just proud, I was jumping-up-and-down proud.

Unfortunately, my second semester was the flip-side of "proud":

English Grammar and Sentence Structure - A

First Aid Responder - D

Kinesiology: Biomechanics and Application - D

Organization of Administration of Physical Education - D

The only reason I didn't flunk out was that my English teacher saw how hard I was working and gave me a chance to earn extra credit. I needed one point to bring my B up to an A, and I got it.

That A boosted me to a 2.0 for the semester, so my six vows were already paying off. And my obvious willingness to work hard helped me create a connection with my English teacher, who made a huge difference by simply believing in me and giving me a chance to succeed.

I ran into Coach Broyles shortly after the second semester ended. He was definitely keeping track of me, and he wasn't especially happy.

"You made 3.0 last semester, Tree, and then followed it up with a 2.0. Whatever happened, you'd better pick up the slack. You made a promise, remember?"

"Yes, sir, Coach. No excuses, and that promise still stands—I'll do my best."

And I meant it.

But the following semester, the fall of 1985, I got another 2.0.

I really had tried, and done my best. Obviously, I couldn't do this by myself anymore. I talked to Coach about it, and he suggested hiring a tutor, a young woman named Marcia Hariell, who was helping Razorback football players with their studies.

Marcia was pleasant and easygoing, the first person who ever took the time to sit down with me, take a personal interest, and try to teach me something. Right from the beginning, I told her I'd arrived on campus illiterate and that I was just now learning how to study.

She was incredulous. "How on earth did you get admitted?"

I told Marcia my whole story. The story of my life, no holds barred. The ups and downs. Growing up poor. Getting passed through one grade after another to stay eligible to play basketball. The disposable life of an NBA player. And she listened to me like no one else ever had.

"Dean," she said when I'd finished telling her everything, "that breaks my heart. So I'll tell you what I'm going to do. I'll give you my total, full-time attention. No other students, just you. I live in a little white house right across from the campus. I'll give you my address, and I'll work with you every day to help you."

I was so grateful, and hopeful for the first time in a while.

The next day I knocked on Marcia's door right on time, eager to get started. She was divorced and lived with her two children, Rob and Mary Robin, both in junior high school, and she introduced us and explained our tutoring arrangement and schedule to them. They seemed like good kids, and it was energizing to just be in that clean, tidy home with that nice, healthy family of three. Marcia was disciplined and serious about this studying thing without being a dictator about it, which made me comfortable right from the jump.

We had our first laugh on the second day, when I showed up with a huge bump on my forehead. She was concerned, maybe afraid I'd been in a fight or something, until I explained that I'd moved into a basement apartment off campus and, since basement apartments aren't known to be kind to 6-feet-9-inch people, I kept hitting my head on the water pipes that ran along the ceiling.

"Bless your heart," Marcia said, genuinely sympathetic for a minute or two, until we both gave in to how ridiculously, harmlessly funny it was.

"Maybe bless that pipe, too, because it might knock some smarts into my hard head," I added.

"We're going to do that ourselves, Dean."

It never ceased to amaze me how much more motivated I was by comments like that than I was by whippings with belts and paddles.

The courses were hard in the spring semester of 1986, but between my efforts and Marcia's help, I was getting the hang of it.

Intermediate English Composition - C

History (1492–1877) - C

Political Science - C

General Psychology - C

Okay, it was only a 2.0, but it kept me enrolled, legitimately, and Marcia and I would make better progress next time. I'd gained a new sense of confidence with her help. It didn't matter how hard the course was, as long as she was there.

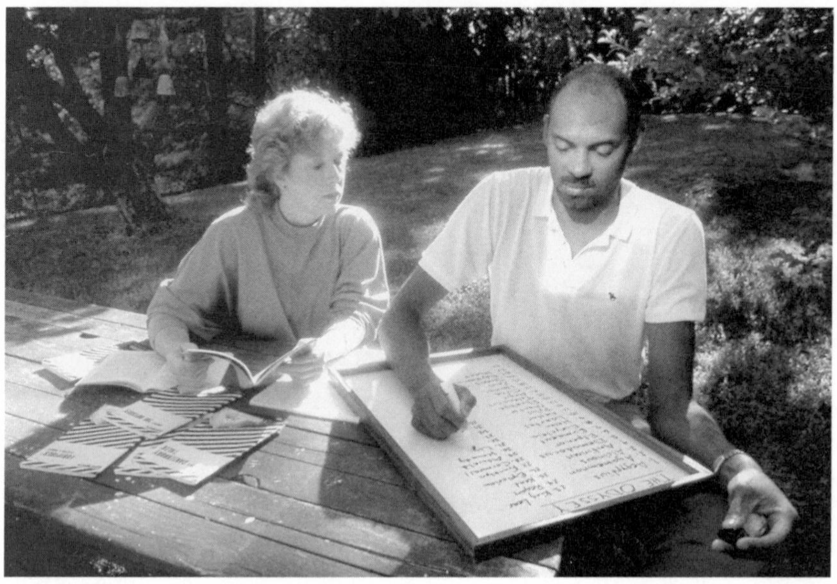

Excellent tutoring was paramount
COURTESY OF *SPORTS ILLUSTRATED*, PHOTOGRAPHER/PHIL HUBER

There was just one problem, and it wasn't a small one—by the fall semester of 1986, I'd run out of money.

Working as hard as I was in school but not having a dime to my name made me very depressed and very discouraged. And what do you know, through my basketball contacts, I heard about a team in Buenos Aires, Argentina, that was hiring. They offered me a contract for $20,000, so I took a hiatus from school and flew to South America.

When I suddenly left campus, everyone thought—and I couldn't really blame them—that I had given up because school was too hard, and I was gone for good. I hadn't even stuck around long enough to explain that my intention was exactly the opposite. I was doing the only thing I could think of that might make it possible for me to come back to school and finish.

Argentina was one of the rougher places I ever played, and the streets were even rougher than the basketball court. In the summer of 1986,

Argentina was in the aftermath of the Falklands War. Great Britain had been fighting over the islands off the Argentinian coast, and the US military got caught up in the conflict. The Argentinians were very angry about that.

In fact, I got chased one night after a game by a bunch of angry Argentinians who wanted to kill me—not because I was Black, but because I was an American. Bad knee and all, I ran for my life while they kept coming, shouting, "You Americans kill our boys! Now we kill you!"

I picked up speed and left my would-be assassins in the dust. Then I ducked into a small bar and called my Argentine coach, Coach Lolo.

"A bunch of guys just tried to kill me," I panted, scared and out of breath.

"What for?"

"They were hollering that we're killing their boys."

His response was as matter-of-fact as it gets. "You are. I mean, the United States is. There's a war going on in the Falklands, in case you didn't know."

"I've just been concentrating on one thing, Coach. My game."

"And you're winning, my friend," he said. "I'll keep you around."

He was right. We were winning. So rather than follow my momentary instinct to jump on a plane and get the hell back to the United States, I'd stick around and complete my commitment to the team. After all, as long as I was taking care of business on the court and outrunning angry mobs, I might even live to graduate.

As planned, I finished the season, got paid, and flew back to Kansas City to see my mother. Her face lit up when I told her I'd made enough money to go back to Arkansas, pay my tutor, and finish my classes.

"Honey, I'm so happy you're going to stick with it!" she told me, beaming.

I wanted to do something nice for her, after a lifetime of her sacrificing for me, so I had her house covered with beautiful vinyl siding that made it look brand new. I even had enough to buy a silver two-door 1985 Buick Park Avenue with a black crushed velvet interior. I'd appreciated my brother's old Grand Prix, but I can't honestly say I was sorry to get rid of it.

Mother's home improvement and my Park Avenue were all paid for, and I still had $7,000 in the bank for school. I'd left Arkansas broke, depressed, and discouraged, but I was going back in much better shape, mentally and financially, in the spring of 1987 for a final attempt at earning my degree.

My first call was to Marcia. I told her I was back from South America and ready to work. Like everyone else, she was pleasantly surprised—she'd wondered if she was ever going to see me again.

Next came a message from Coach Broyles. He wanted to see me immediately. I was sure he did. I stepped into his office, braced for whatever the voice of God in Arkansas had to say.

"Tree," he started, "you made yourself some money overseas?"

"Yes sir, Coach, I did."

"Well, good for you. Now, let's get something straight—I don't want you to leave this campus again until the day you walk across that stage and graduate. Do we understand each other?"

I let out a long exhale, relieved that he hadn't summoned me to his office to say, "Goodbye forever, Tree."

"Yes sir, Coach, absolutely. I'm sorry. I was just broke and needed money really bad."

He studied me briefly. He still wasn't thrilled with me, but he accepted my apology with a simple, "Let's go get you enrolled again."

"Yes sir."

Again, another chance I may not have deserved. After all, I'd left school after promising I wouldn't. But I still had the passing GPA I'd promised, and the money I'd earned in Argentina made a huge difference to both my bank account and my confidence. I also knew Marcia would help me as long as she saw me trying hard to help myself.

I made another change that fall that also made a positive difference. My sister Boni took a look at my transcript and, based on my grades, suggested I change my major from Physical Education, where I wasn't particularly excelling, to History, where I was doing much better. I have no idea why that was true, but it was, and I took Boni's suggestion and changed my major to History.

The more I thought about it, though, the more sense it made to me that I "got" history. To me, it boiled down to four basic things: a date, an event, a name or names, and a place. Put them together in a reasonable way, and you've got a good glimpse of history. Remembering all four gets you an A; three gets you a B; two gets you a C; and one gets you a D. If you remember none, you've got yourself an F.

I often wondered why that was so easy for me when so many other subjects gave me trouble. But through working with Marcia, I discovered that I had a photographic memory. Who knew? A photographic memory—at least mine—works best when it has visual information to capture and hold onto. Of course, other aspects are at play as well. For example, I was much better at learning through phonetic sounds, repetition, talking, spelling, and writing. When there was something specific I needed to learn, I'd write it over and over until my fingers blistered; then I'd pop the blisters and keep on writing.

Thanks to that process, I discovered a kind of magic in writing. If I didn't write something by hand, I wasn't learning. But if I did, my photographic memory captured the fact or historical detail or whatever I was studying, I'd remember it forever, and thanks to that discovery, I brought some of my C grades up to As.

In the spring of 1987, I took Economics, American Negro History, English History (1066–1603), and Western Civilization, and I also learned another thing I'd never known about myself—I was especially good at concentrating in the relaxed, pure, undistracted atmosphere of nature.

Every morning I'd wake up with the sun and go to the park while the grass was still wet with dew and the birds were chirping. Then I'd actually visualize the characters who played a role in forming Western culture and feel myself "enter" them. I'd *become* Zeus, Hercules, Odysseus, Daniel Webster, Horace Greeley, Sir Walter Raleigh, Winston Churchill, Sir Thomas More, anyone and everyone I was reading about. It was amazingly liberating, and exhilarating, to find out that, simply by reading and letting myself get absorbed instead of distracted, I could be any historical character I wanted to be. My imagination was broader than any horizon on earth, and I was putting it to good use. The moment I imagined, I learned. And the moment I learned, I remembered.

Once we got a clear idea of how my mind worked, and didn't, Marcia and I worked hard on perfecting my study techniques. She would read to me, for example, and then have me read the same text back to her. By practicing over and over, I got more and more comfortable dealing with words on a page. She was so thorough and so diligent that she even talked to some of my professors about what areas I needed to concentrate on the most. I'll always credit her tutoring as being a huge part of my success at the University of Arkansas and beyond.

The spring semester of 1987 was by far the most challenging one I'd faced so far. After all, I wasn't taking How to Hit a Golf Ball and Ballroom Dancing anymore. All my courses were the real deal. Marcia was tireless, and so was I—I studied from 12 to 15 hours a day. And what do you know, I was rewarded, or rewarded myself, with a hard-earned, legitimate B in every class and a 3.0 GPA.

I won't forget the handshake I got from Coach Broyles when he saw my grades, and possibly the biggest grin I'd ever seen on his face. "Way to go, son. I'm so proud of you. You're really showing them, aren't you?"

"Yeah, Coach, I am, and it feels great, too."

"You keep up the good work, Tree."

I can honestly say that shaking hands with the man who'd never given up on that tall, immature, illiterate boy he'd met on that same campus all those years ago meant as much to me as any moment I ever had in the NBA, or anywhere else in the world.

Given the countless hours we were spending studying, Marcia asked me to move into the house with her and her kids. In addition to spending almost the entire day working with me, she had them to take care of too, and she thought if I were there full-time when I wasn't in my classes, it would be less disruptive to her household, and I wouldn't have to be shuffling back and forth from the campus and my apartment to her place.

As you might imagine, that arrangement wasn't met with universal approval. Mother was dead set against me sharing a house with a white woman and her children. And when Marcia's father heard about it, he was so angry that a Black man had moved in, he refused to enter the house while I was living there, even to visit his own daughter and grandkids. But in spite of all that drama and all those judgments, Marcia kept right on helping me study every single day, and every single day, I got closer and closer to graduating.

Impossible as it seems looking back on it, my living in that house translated to even more hours of studying. Sometimes Marcia would burn out and go to bed while I'd stay up and keep at it. Some mornings, she'd come scuffing out of her bedroom and find me in front of an open book in the same position she'd left me in the night before. Very often, especially before a test, I'd stay up all night, terrified that I'd forget what I'd studied, and rush straight from her sofa to the classroom to make sure I didn't get amnesia along the way.

In the summer of 1987 I had to take four back-to-back courses. Specifically, I was required to take Algebra to graduate, but I had no math classes on my transcript. Marcia went to the College of Education and talked to them about the math requirements. To our mutual surprise, they told her that I could substitute Math Patterns for Algebra. Math and I had never been friends, but even though Math Patterns was tough, I pulled a solid C. It was my first experience with a math class in my entire academic career that I legitimately passed without just being handed a grade and moved along.

I wasn't necessarily looking forward to it, but I also took Chinese History. I was wrong to have hesitated. It amazed me that so many things I'd assumed were European or American inventions, when I gave them any thought at all, were actually created by the Chinese thousands of years ago. It was realizations like this that upset me about having so stubbornly dismissed school in the first place. I'd learned a lot about the world by playing basketball and living in different cultures, but now I was discovering I'd just scratched the surface.

I also took Social Class in America that semester. I got an A, and one of the reasons for that was because I'd personally experienced poverty, illiteracy, and racial division, and I'd spent a good deal of my life trying to understand why a man's talents depended on his social position, the color of his skin, and the amount of money in his pocket—which was exactly what Social Class in America was about. It explored issues I'd struggled to overcome (and still do, for that matter), primarily the fact that conditions in the American social order favor one class over another (even to this day).

In the summer of 1987, I made a 2.75 GPA.

That fall semester, I signed up for six classes instead of four. I guess I'd been feeling a little too cocky and got myself in way over my head. I had to drop a class—Black Studies Seminar—to keep my GPA from sinking like a rock.

There were times when Marcia and I worked so hard, and I got so stressed out, that I would break down and cry. I knew it wasn't just that none of this was coming easily to me, or the pressure of trying to keep my grades up. It was also built-up frustration from a lifetime of battling against a system that was all too happy to pass me when they needed me and perfectly content to fail me when they didn't.

Crying was often my way of venting that frustration and preventing it from becoming rage. We men are taught not to show vulnerability or weakness; we're supposed to bury it inside of us until it explodes, so there were also times when anger would take over. I'd lash out and rant to Marcia for hours at a time. About how the system had betrayed me. How someone should have noticed I couldn't read or write and seen to it that I learned. How I felt used as a Black athlete. Even, sometimes, how I felt betrayed by my own family. I didn't realize then that I could be my own worst enemy by delving into all that darkness, especially when it came to my family history.

It was tough on Marcia. One day, after I'd raved and cried about everything—being poor, being illiterate, my family, the NBA, you name it—Marcia said we should stop for the day, and she left. She bought herself a milkshake and took a walk in the nearby graveyard, just to cloak herself in some peace and stillness for a while.

When she came back, she patiently helped me understand that blaming others—or myself, for that matter—had nothing to do with where I was and where I'd be going. No good could come from dragging all that baggage from the past around with me. It would do nothing but weigh me down and get in my way, and it wasn't as if I could go back and change a damned thing. If I'd just look around at where I was *now*, how far I'd come, how much I'd learned, and how much I'd grown, I'd be as proud of myself as she was.

What a remarkable woman she was. She had a unique ability to see the best in me, and in others. She couldn't get paid enough to do what she did to help me. There were a few people in my life who'd not just said but shown that they believed in me, and I couldn't let myself use my past as an excuse to disappoint them. Mother. Frank Broyles. And Marcia Hariell.

Ultimately, all the work we put in together paid off handsomely. I ended the spring semester with a 3.75 GPA, and I graduated—*graduated*!—with a 1.93 GPA overall, and 204 cumulative credit hours.

Undergrad ceremony
COURTESY OF *SPORTS ILLUSTRATED*, PHOTOGRAPHER/PHIL HUBER

Somehow or other my story was beginning to make national news. Editors at *Sports Illustrated* thought my long, hard road to graduation, not to mention my long, hard road to the NBA and beyond, was a tale worth telling. In the May 12, 1988, issue, they shared my story with the world in a five-page spread.

It still makes me smile. As a child, I'd dreamed of seeing a photo of myself making a slam dunk on the cover of *Sports Illustrated.* Instead, I wound up in that illustrious magazine with a cap and gown, a bachelor of science in education, and a coaching endorsement that required having at least 60 hours of human anatomy out of 124 hours of coursework.

I can't count the number of times I'd imagined myself walking across that stage to get my diploma. But the night before graduation, I couldn't sleep, tortured by visions of the chancellor holding out my diploma and then snatching it back when I reached for it because of some course I hadn't passed after all, or some test I'd forgotten to take.

Fortunately, that never happened. I walked off the stage with my diploma in my hand and my family right there in the auditorium for the ceremony. The lead-in pictorial in *Sports Illustrated* featured Mother crowning me with my graduation cap, and who deserved it more than she did? She'd loved me all my life, more than anyone else in the world. She'd even risked my wrath by hiding my plane ticket and passport to stop me from flying back to Greece to play another season of basketball and convince me to go back to school and learn to read and write instead. She was the real hero that day, and as far as I was concerned, she was graduating along with me.

When the article came out, Marcia showed it to her dad. She said he told her after he'd read it that helping me was probably the most important thing she'd ever done, and he asked her if I would come see him. I didn't make it there before he passed away, but it makes me happy that he got to see his daughter recognized for the extraordinary person she was, and to see me recognized for what I accomplished with her help. It was nothing short of a miracle.

There was just one piece of business left to take care of:

Now that I had a degree from the University of Arkansas, I finally had the confidence and the credentials to go after what I knew I was destined for at this stage of my life—I was going to be the best damned college basketball coach this country had ever seen.

Chapter Sixteen

I hit the ground running, applying for college coaching positions anywhere and everywhere I might know someone who could put in a good word for me, or even anywhere I might know someone who *knew* someone. Experience? Check. National press? Check. Enthusiasm? Over the top. An avalanche of offers should be coming in any minute now.

One thing I didn't take into account, though, was that my résumé glittered. It's nice to be hot, but my résumé and the *Sports Illustrated* article were almost "too hot to handle, too cold to hold." I was advised by more than one former coach that other coaches would probably be reluctant to hire me because they'd see me as a threat to eventually replace them. I was so hungry for a shot at coaching, and so convinced that I'd be good at it, it didn't occur to me that I might be regarded as a threat rather than an asset.

Then I happened to run into my Arkansas coach, Lanny Van Eman, at the 1988 Final Four in Kansas City's Kemper Arena. I hadn't seen or talked to him in years, so we had lunch together to catch up.

He'd read the *Sports Illustrated* article, and he was beaming at me about it. "I'm so proud of you I don't even know what to say, Tree."

"How about helping me find a coaching job?" I suggested.

His face fell a little. "I'll do what I can, but I'll tell you right now, there aren't a lot of jobs out there."

It was my face's turn to fall when he went on. "The only thing you can hope for is finding an assistant coaching job."

Okay, maybe a small glimmer of hope. "I really think I'd be great at it, Coach."

"No question," he said. "In this tight market, getting a position is hard, but I'll do what I can."

I saw him talking to one of the coaches later that day at the arena about hiring me, and that coach shaking his head no. Really? Just like that, without even interviewing me? I know it was just one guy, but it was so discouraging it hit me hard. I was staying with Uncle Raymond, and I broke down in frustrated tears when I got home that night.

"Why did I go back to college and get my degree if it would turn out not to mean a damned thing?"

"Dean," he smiled, "I worked as a janitor for 40 years. The last five years they made me a security guard because I was too old for mopping and waxing floors. I don't mind what I do. But if I were you, I'd rather shovel shit than beg these coaches for a position at their universities. You know, those guys don't care who you are or what you've done. They never scored 30 points and grabbed 20 rebounds like you did. They never became NBA stars and got written up in any national magazine like you did. For that reason alone, they're not going to hire you."

Uncle Raymond was one of the wisest men I ever knew, and his words carried a lot of weight with me. "This world ain't about bein' fair," he said. "It's about what you *can* do, not about what someone *thinks* you can do. You're a big, tall, hardworking man, and you still got your youth. Why don't you start your own business?"

"Uncle Raymond, I don't want to start my own business. I want to coach!"

He slammed his fist on the table. "Listen to me, son! It ain't gonna happen!"

I went back to Seattle broke as usual, packed up, and moved to Tacoma, where I settled in with my old friend Brian Hardy. The Hardys had been like a second family to me in Seattle, even including me in their holidays, and I knew Tacoma would come to feel like home to me in no time because Brian was like a brother.

Shortly after that move I got an idea about catching hold of one more basketball job through my pal Sanchez in Mexico, who said he'd ask around and get back to me. He did, a week later.

"Dean, I can't promise you're going to make the kind of money you used to make. Right now it's only about 12 grand for a season. You want it?"

No, it wasn't nearly the kind of money I used to make. But it was 12 grand more than I had, so hell yes, I wanted it. I packed my bags and hit the road.

For the next five months, I played basketball in Aguascalientes, Mexico. My knee gave me some problems, but I fought through them because I knew without a doubt that I was playing my last season of professional basketball.

And then, it was over. I was on a plane back to Washington State with $9,000 in my pocket and my lifelong dream in my rear view mirror once and for all.

What now?

Throughout that eight-hour flight, I kept asking myself that question over and over again, and hearing Uncle Raymond's voice over and over again, reminding me, "It's about what you *can* do, not what someone *thinks* you can do." Somewhere along the way, I started putting "what I *can* do" together with the job I'd had for my last two years at the University of Arkansas—I'd cleaned carpets.

I didn't mind a bit doing that kind of work, and I made good money. I saw how the business worked, including the obvious fact that the owner of the company was certainly making more than the $6.50 an hour he was paying us employees. I thought at the time what a great gig that must have been for him. What if I could be that guy? What if I had people working for me, at something I already knew how to do myself? Sure, I'd tried owning a business before, with Lito, and that was a disaster. But it wasn't as if I could have just taken over the tailoring part of the business when he disappeared on me. Besides, I was older and wiser than I'd been then. I'd learned a lot. A whole lot. In fact, I was a college graduate, thank you very much. I could do this now. I felt it. I *knew* it.

This time, I did my research. I opened up a $2,000 line of credit and flew to Indianapolis to visit a place called Bane-Clene, where I could get licensed, bonded, and certified to professionally clean carpets.

I also went to GMAC while I was there, the General Motors credit division, about using the rest of the credit for a down payment on a $40,000 cleaning van. They wouldn't sell me the cleaning van, but they offered me an alternative—a party bus you could rent out and drive around town. It had couches in it for the party-goers to settle in and have sex if the mood, drugs, and alcohol struck them. Maybe the car salesman took a look at me and thought I was more suited to be a pimp than a carpet cleaner.

I convinced them to sell me an empty van, which I took back to Bane-Clene to have them install state-of-the-art carpet cleaning equipment. I even modified some of the equipment myself to make it more portable so I could get more jobs with it.

On the drive back to Washington State, I cleaned carpets for friends and family along the way. And when I got home, I started the first Black-owned carpet-cleaning company in Tacoma. I called it Glow Carpet Glow, inspired by a chicken place down the street from Mother's house in Kansas City called Go Chicken Go.

I had my van decaled with my carpet-cleaning advertisement and my personalized phone number, (253) 752-SCUM. The SCUM stood for "Shampoo, Carpet, and Upholstery Maintenance." There were people who thought I was nuts, but they couldn't deny that the word SCUM got lots of attention.

Before long an article appeared in the *Tacoma News Tribune* about me—the former player from the SuperSonics who'd become a local entrepreneur. When the article came out, I got a cold call from a guy named John McDaniel.

"Beautiful, inspiring story," he said.

"Thank you, sir. Need your carpets cleaned?"

"I've got something more important than that to talk to you about."

I had a business to promote, after all, so, "What's more important than a clean carpet?"

He chuckled at that, and then gave me an answer I couldn't argue with. "I have 3,000 kids ready to sit in an auditorium and hear you tell your story."

"My story?"

"Just tell them how you went back to school, finally learned to read and write, and got your degree. If you'll do that for me, you'll have a friend for life. I can't pay you, but after reading about you, I thought maybe you'd want to do it for the kids."

So thanks to John McDaniel, and three women named Ann Washington, Anna Sacks, and Marie Sallis, who were the founding members of the University Place Black Parents Association, my life as a public speaker and mentor to kids began.

On the day of my speech at Curtis Junior High School, just outside of Tacoma, I was pretty nervous. I'd talked to kids before while doing community work for the Sonics, but never 3,000 kids at the same time. Once I got started, though, I almost couldn't stop. I had so much to say to these kids that the words just poured out of me, and they sat up straight and really listened to every single minute.

I knew I wasn't the only kid in the world who'd hated school, who couldn't read or write, who the system passed along so they could move out into the world and become somebody else's problem. I didn't want those kids to get exploited the way I did, or seduced by a dream that wasn't nearly as thrilling as it looked. I wanted to own up to my mistakes so they might not make some of those mistakes themselves. And the earlier I could help them realize how important education turned out to be, even for a guy who grew up thinking it was the stupidest, most boring waste of time in the history of the universe, the more I could help them.

It was exhilarating, a genuine high point in my life. I gained a friend in Mr. McDaniel, I gave some more talks in the Tacoma area, and I found a passion that continues to give me joy to this very day. I've done public speaking hundreds and hundreds of times since then, all over the country, every chance I've been given.

Unfortunately, not everything else in my life was going quite as smoothly.

It started out as an ordinary evening in 1993. I was driving home from a nightclub called Aztecas in Tacoma with two friends, Larry and Noble. Larry lived on the east side, which was a rough part of town, and it was on the way to drop him off at his house that I heard police sirens behind us and pulled over.

When you were Black and driving a nice car, you got used to being pulled over by white police officers. They'd use any excuse to stop you, search your vehicle, and question you about "how you got this fancy car."

This practice of stopping people for "driving while Black" had started in my hometown of Kansas City many years earlier. Cops were trying to get guns off the street. They didn't have probable cause to search random people just walking around to see if they were armed. But they could find lots of probable causes to pull you over if you were driving. Going five miles per hour over the speed limit. Taillight not working. Sometimes they'd speed up behind you, and if you switched lanes to let them pass but forgot to signal, guess what—you'd just committed a traffic violation, and they'd "need" to search your car.

Pulling people over for . . . whatever . . . seemed to be helping cops confiscate guns in Kansas City and lowering the crime rate, so police departments all over the country began looking for reasons to stop drivers, especially Black ones.

There was nothing routine about my traffic stop in Tacoma that night in 1993. When I pulled over, there were suddenly 12 officers surrounding the car, one of them pressing a 9mm gun to my head. It seems there had been a drive-by shooting somewhere near there a few minutes earlier, and as of right now, I was the prime suspect. If I'd so much as breathed wrong, I might not be here today to tell this story.

I remained calm on the outside, but inside I was more terrified than I'd ever been in my life. "I played for the Seattle SuperSonics," I said without raising my voice, "and I've done nothing wrong tonight."

The cops bent me over the hood of my car, handcuffed me, and put me facedown on the ground. Once they'd searched my BMW and found nothing of any interest, they finally released me. I know beyond the shadow of a doubt that if I'd resisted and fought for my rights, they would have killed me, and there's not a jury in the country that would have convicted them. The only thing I was guilty of was "driving while Black." Had I still been in the NBA, they would have asked me for game tickets and autographs. Instead, they were a trigger-pull away from giving me a death sentence.

As a result of that event, my attorney filed a lawsuit for $3.3 million against the City of Tacoma for an unlawful search. The police—all of them white—lied all the way down the line about what happened that night. I spent seven years fighting for my rights and suing that police department in the judicial system. But what can you do when 12 "officers of the law" swear under oath that they never held a weapon to your head?

The case was documented in court and was initially thrown out on a summary judgment, meaning there was a judgment with no trial, and just like that, it was as if it had never happened. The cops, who'd essentially won, were very poor sports about the whole thing and kept doing drive-bys past my house to harass me, yelling, "We told you to leave it alone, Nigga!" I began to fear for my safety all over again. It wasn't until I spoke to Tacoma mayor Bill Baarsma that the police harassment stopped.

The story attracted national television attention on a program called *A Current Affair*. It even went all the way to the US Supreme Court. I contacted Gerry Spence about my case. He was a brilliant trial attorney who'd made a name for himself taking on major corporations, as he had for Karen Silkwood, the highly publicized whistleblower at a plutonium production plant whose story was told in a Meryl Streep movie called *Silkwood.*

Gerry Spence was sympathetic and a great listener, but he finally asked me the definitive question: "Do you have $500,000 to lose if you don't win, Dean? Because that's how much it would cost to get your case in front of the Supreme Court."

End of discussion, end of a case I'd spent seven years fighting for, even though the truth was 100 percent on my side. Now that nearly everyone on the planet is equipped with cellphone video cameras, footage of police abuse appears on the news almost daily and continues to make me break out in a sweat of relief at how lucky I was to have survived that night, and mourn for those victims whose only crime was having the "wrong" color skin.

As common as it is for all of us to worry about the future, there are times when I'm grateful we don't know what's coming. I can't imagine how much time and energy I would have wasted on worrying if I'd known I had an arrest by the Tacoma Police Department to look forward to . . . or yet another lawsuit to look forward to once that case was over with.

Somehow, while all of that was going on, my carpet-cleaning business was moving right along. According to a US Department of Commerce report I'd read, most Black-owned businesses failed during the first two or three years. "Most" didn't mean "all," and I wasn't about to fall into some statistically predicted doom.

In its first year, my business grossed $24,000, and it kept on going so well that after a couple of years, I decided to expand. I applied for a loan from Seattle First National Bank in Tacoma with the assistance of the branch manager Bob Peterson, who told me that if I could land a bigger contract, the bank could loan me more money.

Enough said. I went straight to the procurement office of the biggest company in the area—Boeing—and picked up the paperwork for a cleaning bid. My friend John McDaniel helped me do the number crunching; and bidding against 13 other vendors, I won the $1.2 million contract for their carpet-cleaning services.

Bob Peterson was astonished. "You actually went out and got it!" But when he looked over the contract, he lost some of that enthusiasm.

"Dean, this is too large a contract for a company that only has one truck."

Well, that was an easy one to solve. "Then I'll just go out and buy more vehicles and equipment. What's the problem?"

He sat there shaking his head. "The problem is, if you take a contract this large, your company is guaranteed to fail. I can't justify lending you that kind of money on a contract you can't possibly satisfy. Maybe you can go back to Boeing and ask if you could take care of, let's say, one or two plants rather than the whole company."

I gave it a try, and Boeing said yes. They awarded me the contract for their Auburn Fabrication Plant, which was near my house in Tacoma. They paid $500,000 for the first year, with a $500,000 extension on the second year and a $100,000 carpet repair contract as well.

Altogether, that made it almost a $1.2 million contract over two years instead of one.

I'd also continued to enjoy my speaking engagements in and around Tacoma. Mayor Baarsma attended a number of them and witnessed firsthand how they impacted the kids and young people in the community. In 2003, he honored me with a proclamation and key to the city of Tacoma, Washington, for my contribution to the students in the Tacoma school district. I treasure that key to the city as much as any accolade I ever received from playing basketball. It meant I was helping people. It meant I was making a difference, and there's no feeling in the world, bar none, that can ever top that.

Although I have to say, working hard for your money and knowing you earned every dime of your paycheck ranks right up there, and that's exactly what I intended to do at Boeing. I hadn't realized until I started what a poor job the previous vendor had done, and shame on them for that. I couldn't even begin to get those carpets clean until I'd removed all the soap they'd left behind, which took forever.

But that wasn't the only problem. My point person at the Boeing facility apparently hadn't been told how much I was making, and she was appalled when she found out.

"$25,000 a month?!" she practically shrieked. "We can't pay you that! Our plant manager doesn't even make that much money!"

I'd already cleaned hundreds of thousands of square feet of carpeting for them. Bob Peterson, the bank manager, was even helping me at night. And she was implying that I hadn't earned what my contract clearly spelled out?

I never considered a job complete until I'd asked the customer if they were satisfied. I can still picture the disgusted look on that point person's face when she marched me past the vast expanse of sparkling clean carpet I'd given them and pointed to three pieces of fossilized gum, buried in a corner, that had probably been stuck in that carpeting since dinosaurs roamed the planet.

Long story short—they tried to break the contract. I filed a lawsuit. I inadvertently hired a lawyer who had no business practicing law and, for all I know, was trying to make a good impression on Boeing and gave me terrible advice in court, and the case went on for four years until it was settled through mediation.

This was my first experience with corporate America, and my first lesson in the fact that, among countless other revelations, they play by their own rules. I had massive monthly payments on the money I'd borrowed, and of course Boeing wasn't about to pay me while we were in litigation, so whatever money I was making on other jobs was being drained off by my overhead.

Finally, to keep my head from exploding, I decided I needed to get away for a few days to clear my head and figure out what to do next, and I took off for Kansas City to visit my mother. On the way, my car broke down, and, as if it was meant to be, I got a lift from a nice family, the father of whom happened to be an insurance attorney.

As we drove along, I spilled my whole sad story about losing the Boeing contract. "Dean," that nice man said, "what you need is a lawyer who sues other lawyers. That's what I do in Portland, and I know someone who could help you."

He gave me his contact's information, and I resolved to proceed when I got back to Washington. The way it worked out, my new attorney filed papers for the termination of my contract against the original lawyer who had made so many mistakes and omissions. That lawsuit went on for several years while I kept cleaning carpets and running my business. In the end, I got a settlement for a fraction of what the trucks and carpet-cleaning equipment cost me, and my business continued to run in the red.

But for the next 10 years, I kept chiseling away at that debt, and through a lot of prayers, tears, and hard work, I kept the business afloat. There was no job too small, too hard, or too big. I worked almost every night and every weekend. It was backbreaking work.

Then, I nearly broke my back.

I'd been playing in legends games every year with the Sonics. It was a fun way to stay in touch with former teammates and raise money for good causes. It was during a benefit game for the US Senior Citizens Olympic Games, sponsored by the Seattle SuperSonics, at Saint Martin's

University in Olympia, Washington, that I hurt my back so badly I became permanently disabled. I remember jumping in the air as high as I could, attacking the basket, and getting bridged by a player. I hit the floor on my back, and I was in so much pain I blacked out. The next thing I knew, I was in the ICU, where I was diagnosed with a bulging herniated disc, L-4 and L-5, with a disrupted sciatica nerve, which left me temporarily paralyzed from the waist down. I was 50 years old, playing against guys who were half my age. My decades of playing basketball on slippery wooden floors had taken their toll. My former teammate Talvin Skinner, a year younger than I was, tore his Achilles tendon in that same game.

Basketball had taken so much out of me, and now it was taking away my ability to work and earn a living. I essentially spent the next two years of my life lying on the floor. For a while, some of my close, loyal friends like Bob Peterson helped fill in for me on jobs. G. Simpson, another Black businessman in Tacoma, helped me as well and became one of my best friends. When I could, and when they needed me, I would prop myself up on a stool and tell my crew what to do on particularly tough, complicated jobs. But eventually it became too much for them, and for me.

It was probably inevitable that as time went on, the business I'd done everything in my power to keep afloat kept taking on more and more water. Between the debt from my battle with Boeing and my back injury, I refinanced my little house eight times. But after 13 long years of carpet cleaning, I'd had it. The bank was trying to foreclose on my house. I ended up selling the business, including the van and all the equipment, to a former employee of mine so that I could cover the bank note, and then I filed for bankruptcy.

At the age of 52, I had to start all over again. Again.

Chapter Seventeen

Starting your life over from square one is tough enough. Starting over when your back is in such pain you're literally crawling back and forth to the bathroom is an overwhelming challenge. Since I could barely care for myself, getting a job was out of the question, so there wasn't a lot to do from one day to the next but lie there and think.

I wondered more times than I could count if I would have dreamed of being a professional athlete if I'd been warned about the toll it was likely to take on my body. I probably would have—when you're young, strong, 6-foot-9 and 200 pounds, your body's a gift, you're immortal, and debilitating injuries only happen to guys who don't know enough to keep themselves in shape.

I'd played four times in five nights for the Sonics. Each time I got down to the low post on offense, I had some guy, usually three to five inches taller and 40 pounds heavier than me, slamming a forearm into my lower back to move me a few inches farther from the basket. I might have to jump 90 or 100 times a night, with adrenalin-charged elbows trying to stop me, to go for rebounds, block shots, or shoot the ball. Every jump and landing forced my lower back to act like a shock absorber. Then, when the game was over, it was on to the first flight out the next morning, cramming my big bruised, battered body into a coach seat for however many hours it took to get to the next city on the schedule.

Of course, in my case, there were also the Greyhound bus accident and the series of spinal taps and God knows what else from God knows how many fights. So I guess it shouldn't have come as a surprise that I'd ended up with the L4 and L5 vertebrae in my back looking as if they were naturally fused together, and that the legends game for Seattle turned out to be the straw that broke my back.

I was seriously considering back surgery, but Mother was dead set against it.

"I work in a hospital," she pointed out. "Honey, once they cut your back open, you'll be in a wheelchair for the rest of your life. I see it happen all the time. It can leave you paralyzed, and you'll never walk again."

I already couldn't walk, but the "paralyzed" thing terrified me, and it wasn't as if arthroscopic surgery was readily available at the time. Back surgery wasn't just a few small incisions and a robot to take care of you. It was a doctor filleting you open and hoping he could fix the problem, kind of like a plumber sawing a hole in your bedroom wall and hoping he can find the leaky pipe.

Finally, in desperation, I called Woody Wouldrop, the team doctor for the Anchorage Northern Knights where I played in the CBA. He was one of the few guys I trusted when it came to injuries, and whatever advice he had to offer, I was ready to follow it.

I explained my situation, and he replied instantly, "Dean, come up here and I'll help you. You can stay at my house."

And just like that, I was being wheeled onto an Alaska Air flight. I kneeled facing the back of the seat while they buckled me in, I was in too much pain to even change positions, and I flew to Anchorage on my knees.

I stayed with Woody for two months while he gave my back all the chiropractic treatments he could. Eventually, he got me to a point where I could at least stand up and take a few steps. I worked my way up to walking for a block before I had to stop. It beat the hell out of lying on my living room floor with the urinal I'd finally invested in to keep from having to crawl all the way to the bathroom.

As I promised Woody I would, I went to the VA hospital to be reexamined when I got back to Tacoma. They strongly urged surgery, and I strongly refused to be cut open, so they did what they decided was the next best thing—they prescribed hydrocodone, a powerful opiate, to help ease the pain.

I was so grateful for the possibility of relief that I didn't think to ask if hydrocodone was addictive, and they didn't think to warn me about it. All I cared about was the idea of living a few hours at a time with a low enough pain level to move around my house and try to get back enough strength to start living my life again.

The common belief about hydrocodone and other opioids is that they make the pain go away. They don't. They just mask the pain and make your brain foggy enough to keep you from thinking about it every minute of every hour of every day. The first time I took my prescription pills, I took three at once, and it was like being asleep while I was still awake. With my brain not involved enough to intervene, I got busy vacuuming the floor I'd practically been living on, and cooking for myself for the first time in a while. My back ached afterwards, of course, but a few more pills and I was okay again.

And that's how quickly the vicious cycle of addiction began. The more the pills masked the pain, the more I was able to do, and the more I was able to do, the more I needed a couple of pills to mask the pain again. I'd take two pills in the evening, more than my prescribed dosage, so I'd have a chance of sleeping through the night, and three pills in the morning so I could cook another meal and straighten up the house.

By 2007, I was surviving, but I wasn't living. I'd hit a wall in my life, seemingly with nowhere to go.

I was too old, and my body was too messed up for me to play basketball anymore.

I couldn't restart my carpet-cleaning company—the work was too grueling for my disabilities to tolerate.

I couldn't become a basketball coach, or even an assistant coach, because they didn't want me.

I had to find a new path to move forward in my life. If you're not growing, you're dying, and I wasn't ready to die.

I'd seen so many guys I played ball with not make it this far. Bill Robinzine committed suicide because of financial problems and an inability to "reconcile not being in the NBA anymore"; John Brisker disappeared in Uganda and was legally declared dead in 1985; even my old teammate Dennis Johnson, three years younger than I was, died of a heart attack earlier in 2007. I was lucky to still be around, but I couldn't let myself just sit there waiting to not be around anymore.

I thought a lot about what I'd accomplished in my life and what I was proud of. The answer I kept coming back to surprised me. More than the NBA, more than playing basketball around the world, more than starting my own company, it was my college degree. Going from an illiterate adult to a college graduate.

Then I saw a statistic that opened my eyes: Less than 1 percent of all Americans earn a master's degree. What if I went back to school and tackled that? How much would it mean to me if I could be part of that "less than 1 percent"? And how much would it mean to Mother?

That settled it—I picked up the phone and called the man who'd helped me graduate from college in the first place, Frank Broyles, who was still the athletic director at the University of Arkansas.

"I'm stuck in my life, Coach," I told him. "Maybe getting a master's degree is what I need to find a new path."

It touched me and motivated me that he sounded so thrilled. "Dean, that's wonderful! Just wonderful! Come on down, and let's get started!"

My hydrocodone, my back, and I flew to Fayetteville, where I was immediately told that the university would not let me into graduate school. Two department heads strongly opposed it, due to my 1.93 undergraduate GPA. The odds were against me, but sorry, been there, done that, not paying attention to the odds anymore. I had nothing left to lose, and failure wasn't an option.

So I stayed on top of them and pleaded my case. In the end, a department head named Dr. Greenwood presented their offer: I needed to take 12 credits, and in the first five classes I took, I'd have to pull a 3.5 GPA or the department would drop me from the master's program. Period. Simple as that. Take it or leave it.

I still remember sitting at that long table in the University of Arkansas conference room. One Dean among a bunch of deans. I shook my head, letting them think for a second that it was too big a challenge for me. Then I announced, "Scratch the 3.5 business. I'm going to make a 4.0."

A few of them rolled their eyes. A few of them looked out the window. All of them joined in a chorus of negative sighs. I didn't care. I knew myself better than they did.

I signed up for two classes, a full load in the master's program. By the end of that first semester, I had As in both courses.

The two deans in the Department of Education who had opposed me still had their hearts set on getting me to drop out. One of them, Dr. O. K. Park, gave me a particularly hard time.

"Why do you think you need this master's degree, Dean?"

"Why did you think you needed yours, Dr. Park?"

"I wanted to get my doctorate," he answered with thinly disguised condescension.

I didn't engage, I just responded with a simple, "So what makes you think I don't want to get *my* doctorate?"

He bristled and shook his head. Unfortunately, Dr. Park was my academic counselor and, stuck with me, he suggested courses for me to take that were extremely difficult. When I spoke to other people in the department, though, they explained that Dr. Park could make all the suggestions he wanted, but he didn't have the authority to force me to follow his advice.

Mind you, none of this was easy, including being in school again. My back pain wasn't going away, and I was up to six hydrocodone tablets a day. But pain or no pain, I hadn't come all this way to quit and go home. I was going to get my master's.

The first semester, I got an A in all three of the education courses I took, which completed my 12-credit-hours trial period. I had a 4.0 GPA and, based on our agreement, the university administrators couldn't kick me out of the program.

But when I didn't fail to meet their expectations as they'd hoped, they went to Plan B and tried to change the rules of the game. This time, they complained that my education was costing the college too much money. That's when Coach Broyles stepped up for me.

"You seem to be forgetting that I get 51 percent of the votes in this department," he reminded them. "He's earned a 4.0 so far, and I say he stays."

After that meeting, Coach Broyles sat down with me and filled me in on what they'd tried to do. He also made a promise to me. "As long as you get good grades, the university will cover your expenses and tuition." No one else at the University of Arkansas seemed to want me there, but he did, and he was the only one who mattered. His commitment to my education, and to me, was second to none.

Then a stroke of pure luck came my way—my counselor Dr. O. K. Park retired. Replacing him was an African-born administrator, scholar, and counselor, Dr. Nafuhko, who became an immediate ally and advocate.

I took a course in AP English and another in English as a Second Language (ESL). I chose to link that with Spanish rather than another language because of my vagabond basketball travels in South America and Mexico. (I never did quite get the hang of the language in the Philippines.)

When the fall semester came along, so did Computer Technology, and it became my nemesis. I was afraid it would derail me, because I had no training in computer science. But there to save the day and have my back as always was my friend and tutor Marcia Hariell. She and I burned gallons of midnight oil for that class, and thanks to her I learned the half-dozen software programs that the course required. I sweated it out, and I ended up with an A.

The final frontier, the only thing standing between graduation and me, was a dreaded course called Research Methods in Statistics Education. I had exactly zero math skills, let alone a course that required *advanced* math skills.

I was right up front with the professor, Dr. Roberts, in a meeting in her office before the class started. "I should explain that I never passed a math class, except for Math Patterns, when I got my undergraduate degree."

She leaned forward, rested her chin on the palm of her hand, and softly, without judgment, asked, "How the hell did you ever get to this level of education?"

"Basketball, to begin with. But as you know, advanced math wasn't required for graduation in 1988."

Then, although I tried to hold them back, tears started rolling down my cheeks. I sat there crying like a baby, believing all the years of struggle had suddenly landed hard on my head. And a strange thing happened—Dr. Roberts got up from her desk, walked around to where I was staring at my feet trying to pull myself together, and gave me a big hug.

"I want you to stop crying so I can tell you how you're going to pass this class."

Her voice was so gentle and reassuring that I raised my head and looked her in the eye.

"The first thing is," she said quietly, "this is not a math class."

She went back to her desk, opened a drawer, and held up a tape measure. "Have you ever used one of these before?"

"Yes, ma'am, I have."

Still in the kindest, softest voice, she explained, "Well, this is a measuring class, not a math class. We're going to learn how to measure things." She pulled out a few inches of the tape, held it, and showed it to me. "Now, tell me what you see on this tape where my thumb is."

"I see one inch."

"What's next?" she asked, moving her thumb.

"One fourth."

She moved it again. "And here?"

"One half."

One more time. "Here?"

"Three fourths."

"Now, there are rules that apply to measurements in statistics: ordinal, nominal, interval, and ratio. They correspond naturally to what you just observed, and they're used to prove a hypothesis. It's all a matter of measurement. Let's prove a hypothesis. How tall are you?"

"Six feet nine inches," I said, actually getting kind of interested in this demonstration.

"Okay, let's find out right now how tall you are relative to all the other men in the United States. Without running the numbers, I can tell you it's over 95 percent."

"How do you know that?"

She smiled. "I've been doing this for more than 30 years, Dean. So what measurement would you use to run this experiment—ordinal, nominal, interval, or ratio?"

"Ratio," I quickly answered.

She was pleasantly surprised. "How did you know that?"

"Well," I said, "I've never heard of those other three." That made her laugh a little. "But I have heard people talk about ratio. It's how much of one thing compares to another thing."

She was so pleased you would have thought I'd just won the final round on *Jeopardy*. "You see, right there, you're correct. You'd use ratio for your height comparison to the other men living in the United States, and that proves your hypothesis. You're going to do fine in this class. Just get an appropriate tutor and work hard."

I walked out of Dr. Roberts's office with a renewed feeling of confidence. I kept repeating my mantra and my prayer as I left the building: *You're going to graduate with a master's degree.*

I asked around, and the next day I called a tutor who'd been recommended for this particular course. He was a graduate student named Scott who was teaching undergraduate statistics and studying for his doctorate in statistics. I told him the shortest possible version of my story, which left him wide-eyed and incredulous. After a long, deep breath as if he were about to try cliff-diving for the first time, he squared his shoulders and smiled right at me.

"Okay, Dean. Let's get started, and get ready to remember stuff. There will be many terms you'll have to know so you can solve the problem when you see it. There are two main parts to statistics—the vocabulary, and running the numbers. Knowing the vocabulary is important. Otherwise you won't be able to run the numbers. I'll teach you how the numbers work and how to solve a statistical hypothesis. Clear so far?"

He left me that evening with a list of words to study and have memorized the next day, with the reminder, "You won't be able to look at a vocabulary list of terms when you're taking the test."

Needless to say, studying was intense, and the hours were long. Scott would study with me for seven hours a day. Then he'd leave and I'd keep going for another 10. That sounds unbelievable, but it's true. I may not have been born to study, but I was born competitive. It was that competitive drive that got me to the NBA, to owning my own business, to graduating college at 36 years of age. When given a challenge, I have an almost superhuman capacity to complete it, whatever it takes.

But sitting for hours upon hours wasn't conducive to diminishing back pain. Instead, it was very effective at raising my pain levels, which required more painkillers, which made me a full-blown opiate addict. The statistics course took five months to complete, but as we continued to study, the work got harder, my pain intensified along with my addiction, and it was all taking its toll.

Halfway through the course, Great Scott (my nickname for my brilliant, tenacious tutor) stopped by my house for a scheduled tutoring session, and I was panicked.

"Great Scott, I can't remember anything you've taught me so far," I confessed.

"You're kidding me, right?"

I shook my head. Scott knew I had severe back pain, but he didn't know about the pills.

"What are you telling me, Dean? You have an exam coming up in two days. How could you blank out everything I've taught you? You've memorized it, you and I have worked our asses off, you've worked *your* ass off . . ."

All I had to offer was a barely audible, "I know, I know. It's just that . . . Scott, my head hurts so bad, I can't think."

"Can you take some meds for that?"

"Already have."

He studied me for a full minute and concluded, "Look, I'm not even going to tutor you today. You focus all your attention on that vocabulary. I'll go visit Dr. Roberts and find out as much as she'll tell me about what's on the test."

He left. I stared at the vocabulary papers. They might as well have been written in Greek. Out of desperation, I swallowed two Vicodin tablets instead of the one I usually took, thinking that might help. I couldn't have been more wrong—they only made things worse. Now my head didn't just hurt, it felt as if Thor was bashing it with his legendary iron hammer. But setting those pages aside and taking a break wasn't an option. I had two days to get ready for a test that would make or break the rest of my life.

I tried so hard to blast through my aching brain fog and study that day, but it seemed that the more I remembered, the less I knew, and the more I knew, the less I remembered. I was exhausted, done in, wiped out, and by 3:00 a.m. I couldn't go on anymore. I shoved all those vocabulary papers under my pillow, terrified that I'd look back on that as the moment I gave up on my future. I was lost, with nothing left except God.

I got on my knees like Granny had taught me to do all those decades ago, said the Lord's Prayer, and then begged God to open my mind and help everything come back that Scott had worked so hard to help me learn. "Without doing well on this test, I'll never get my degree," I prayed out loud. "And God, you have my word, if you'll get me through this, I'll put that degree to good use, doing Your work for the rest of my life."

I crawled into bed and, in spite of my aching back and my aching head, fell sound asleep.

The next morning, the instant I opened my eyes, I felt something come over me, a silent message from His spirit to mine, the simple words, "*Dean. Have no fear.*"

A peaceful, refreshed feeling washed over me. It was as if I'd been transformed from a pill-craving, pain-wracked sufferer to a strong, confident, clear-headed servant of God. I'd prayed countless times, through countless crises, but I don't remember ever getting such an immediate, miraculous message.

I told Great Scott about it, and how I believed, truly believed, that my memory hadn't just come back to me, it was *given* back to me. He listened, put his hand on my shoulder, and said, "If any of my students ever come to me again complaining that they can't do the work to pass a test in my class because it's too hard, I'm going to tell them about the student who never took math and passed this test. I'm going to tell them the Dean Tolson story."

I took the test, and I scored a 97. I trembled when I saw that grade.

Marcia, my loyal tutor, called it "a double miracle—you grasped the material, and you aced the exam! Congratulations, Dean, I'm so happy for you!"

Great Scott literally jumped in the air. "We did it! We did it! Together!" Then he gave me a hug and said, "You're the man!," and I *felt* like *the man*.

I started to cry, but he wasn't having it. "Wipe those tears away, Dean. Now the hard part begins. I'm going to teach you how to run the experiments. Are you ready for this, or do you need a day to rest?"

"I'm ready," I grinned through my tears. "Let's do this."

The second half of statistics consisted of a nonstop barrage of things like an independent t-test; a chi-square test; a Pearson-r test; a Nova, or Null experiment . . . questions that made no sense to me. Just sitting there listening to them was like an out-of-body experience. All I could do was to keep following instructions, little by little, and thinking, "Wow, look at me, the guy they let dribble his way through school with Fs, and now I'm actually *doing* it!"

I was nothing short of euphoric. But lurking beneath the surface of that euphoria like a dark cloud was a fact I kept trying like hell to deny:

That brush with memory loss wasn't exhaustion, or pressure, or head and back pain.

It was opiates.

And if I was going to live long enough to get this master's degree and keep that promise I made to God, I had to face my addiction and put it behind me, no matter what it took.

Chapter Eighteen

I had two choices: live with the pain in my back, or live with the pain of failing my final exam in May of 2007. It wasn't even a close call—no way could I live with failing that final exam, and let down my mother, Coach Broyles, Marcia, Great Scott, and most of all, myself. In order to pass that test, I had to be in the best mental and physical condition of my life, and the one thing that could ruin me at that point was my damned addiction.

In April, I stopped taking Vicodin, cold turkey. It wasn't easy, but after three weeks, I was off drugs. In constant pain, but off drugs.

Inevitably, the day came when I started sweating profusely. I felt lightheaded and wanted to throw up. Suddenly, I couldn't walk and collapsed on the carpet, shaking, my heart trying to beat itself out of my chest. Between muscle contractions and agonizing spasms, I desperately wanted to just pass out.

I closed my eyes. When I opened them again, somehow Satan's voice was silently talking to me, mocking me.

"Look at you, lying there on the floor squirming like a pig in mud. Where's your God now, big boy? Face it, you got nobody. *Nobody*. You need me. You know you do. So surrender and come to me. Now, boy. I command you."

It might have been some kind of withdrawal-induced auditory hallucination, but it was real to me, and I could only think of one way to defend myself from it—I started saying the Lord's Prayer. Satan kept talking over the prayer, so I kept talking louder and louder to drown him out and let him know that he might as well get the hell out of my life, because God and I were in this together and always would be.

Before long I was shouting the Lord's Prayer at the top of my lungs, so loudly that my frightened neighbors managed to get to me and rush me to the nearest emergency room.

After examining me, a stern doctor explained that what I'd just gone through was intense opioid withdrawal. "Don't ever try to detox yourself again. You could have gone into cardiac arrest and died," he informed me. "You need professional help to clear your body of opiates. That was a very dangerous thing you tried to do. Your doctor never warned you about the danger of self-detoxing from addictive drugs?"

"No, sir, he did not."

He scribbled on a prescription pad while explaining, "I'm giving you medication to relax, and then you're going back on Vicodin. You'll stay on them until you can be professionally detoxed, do you understand?"

I nodded and walked out with the prescription he handed me. The medication helped, and I started feeling better right away, so much better that I was able to get back to the grind of studying. The date of the final exam was closing in on me, but my confidence was slowly seeping back into me too.

Until I got a call from my academic adviser Dr. Nafuhko.

"Dean, since you haven't mentioned it, I just wanted to make sure you know about your master's thesis."

Never heard of it. "My what?"

"You choose five topics out of eight to write about, and it has to be completed by the end of the semester. It's the only way you can get your degree."

My heart stopped. Why was I just now hearing about this? It turned out that everyone who was working with me assumed it was common knowledge, and/or that someone else had already discussed it with me. I'd been blindsided by my own ignorance . . . again.

I asked around until I understood the drill. It didn't ease my mind one bit. I'd become pretty good at expressing my thoughts on paper, but I wasn't good at writing APA style, the style required by the American Psychological Association. Somehow I was supposed to come up with a 40-page essay, in a style I struggled with, on subject matter I'd have to research, and still squeeze in enough time to study for the statistics final.

For a moment or two, it flashed through my mind that I could bypass the thesis for the time being and focus all my energy on preparing for the statistics final. Yeah, that would work. Sure, it would mean I may never graduate. And walking across that stage without my diploma. And returning to the University of Arkansas later . . . whenever . . . to write the thesis. Essentially telling the university, "Thanks for the investment you made in me, sorry you caught me at such an inconvenient time."

No way. Not an option. Whatever it took, if it was humanly possible, or even if it wasn't, I had to do this.

So instead of studying 16 or 17 hours a day, I studied 20 hours a day for the rest of April and the beginning of May. I was getting maybe three or four hours of sleep a night, addicted to opiates, dealing with my crushing back injury, and struggling with my literacy problems. I was preparing for a final exam in a course that stumps most *good* students while gathering research for my master's thesis in education and answering tough questions in perfect APA style with the help of the *APA Manual.* Critical writing with a focus on spelling, punctuation, capitalization, italics, abbreviations, proper attribution of references, as well as mathematical copy, headings, tables, and illustrations in the text. Definitely not a manual I would ever pick up again for leisure reading.

There were times when I yearned for my old ACT/SAT tests genius Poindexter, who'd ushered me into the University of Arkansas the first time around. But even he would have been no help—Dr. Nafuhko had me sign an academic honesty agreement stating I would not cheat or have someone help me with my thesis.

No, it was all on me. However this turned out, I'd have to own it. To help prop myself up from time to time, I'd think about my basketball years. I was the guy who wanted to play against the toughest guys the league had to offer. I was the guy who wanted the ball in my hands to take the final shot before the last buzzer. I was the guy who was too competitive to fold under pressure. So now, I might not be wearing a jersey and sneakers, but the ball was in my hands, the buzzer was about to go off, and it was up to me, hit or miss, to take that last shot.

I chose my five topics, wrote them up, and crossed my fingers. Not surprisingly, statistics was not one of the five I chose. I sweated out writing that thesis one agonizing page at a time, never quite sure which was winning—my fear of tying all the loose ends together of the subjects at hand, or the words that were coming out of me as best I could, "best" being the least I'd settle for.

I finished the thesis, turned it in, and crossed my fingers. Meanwhile, Great Scott came and went during the day, giving me pointers and assignments to get me ready for that final statistics exam.

And then it was game time.

I walked into the classroom and sat down, confident that I'd done all I could to get ready for this, without a doubt one of the most defining moments of my life. I took a deep breath to tell my nerves to please stop freaking out, and I looked at the test.

At first glance, I saw the statistical problem. There was also a mathematical problem, followed by this: *Look at the mathematical equation and figure out if the level of measurement is ordinal, nominal, interval, or ratio. Then choose the proper experiment and plot it on the bell curve to prove your hypothesis.*

What?!

Frozen like a deer in the headlights, I felt as if I'd been blindsided. All along, Dr. Roberts had been giving us the instruments, the level of measurement, and the random numbers to plot answers on the bell curve. We hadn't done it this way all semester. I'd worked so hard . . . ! How, and why, would she trick me like this?! I could feel every ounce of confidence, and the rest of my life, slipping away, and I started crying.

Before long Dr. Roberts walked by and slipped a note on my desk. It read something like this: "Work through the ones you know, then come back and work on the ones you don't. Even if you choose the wrong instrument or level of measurement, I'll still give you credit for working the problem all the way through. So get busy and stop wasting time."

Thanks to that note, I composed myself, got control of my fear, stopped shivering, and went to work. It seemed as if only a few seconds passed before Dr. Roberts was moving through the classroom collecting the tests.

I was done and, I prayed, not done in.

Now all I had to do was keep from jumping out of my skin while I waited for two verdicts to come in: the evaluation of my master's thesis, and my final grade in statistics.

The statistics exam grade came back first. A disappointing 65. I'd scored a 97 on the first exam and a 95 on the second one, so I had an A going into the test. But that 65 lowered my grade to a B. Still good enough, and I was almost weak with relief when I went to Mrs. Roberts's office to apologize for my poor performance on the final and to thank her for being such a great teacher.

"I'll never forget that first day in your office, when you helped me understand 'ordinal, nominal, interval, and ratio' by comparing my height to the other men in the United States. It made sense, and I promise I got it, so why I had trouble keeping it straight on that final exam I have no idea. You came through for me every step of the way, I just wish I'd done a better job of coming through for you when I ended up with a B . . ."

She stopped me, smiling. "Dean," she said, "you didn't end up with an A, but I have to say you know something about statistics now, and no one worked harder than you did. I'm proud of you."

Hearing her say that felt better to me than getting an A, and I told her so, from the bottom of my heart.

I had to wait until right before graduation to find out about the thesis evaluation, and it was excruciating, wondering if I'd fail at the last minute and still be one of the 99 percent of Americans who don't get a master's degree.

My damned phone kept not ringing, so I took a walk around campus one day in the hope that it would help relax me a little.

It did, but not at all in the way I expected.

I happened to run into Dr. Nafuhko, and he didn't mince words:

"Dean, you got five out of five committee members giving you a thumbs-up for graduation. Congratulations."

I'm not even sure I thanked him—I was so thrilled I couldn't speak.

Imagine this: I had just become the first functionally illiterate professional athlete to go back to college at 32, repeat four years of undergraduate study, return at age 52, and graduate with a master's degree at the age of 57 *in the top tenth of my class—magna cum laude*! An A in that statistics class would have elevated me to *summa cum laude*, the highest possible distinction, but believe me, at that point I was too blown away to care.

The *cum laude* recognition was formalized with a certificate from the National Honor Society in Chicago, Illinois.

Next came some overwhelming surprises from Coach Broyles:

He was retiring my jersey number.

I was going into the University Hall of Fame.

And he was inaugurating the Dean Tolson Comeback Scholarship Award, to be presented to an athlete on a scholarship at the University of

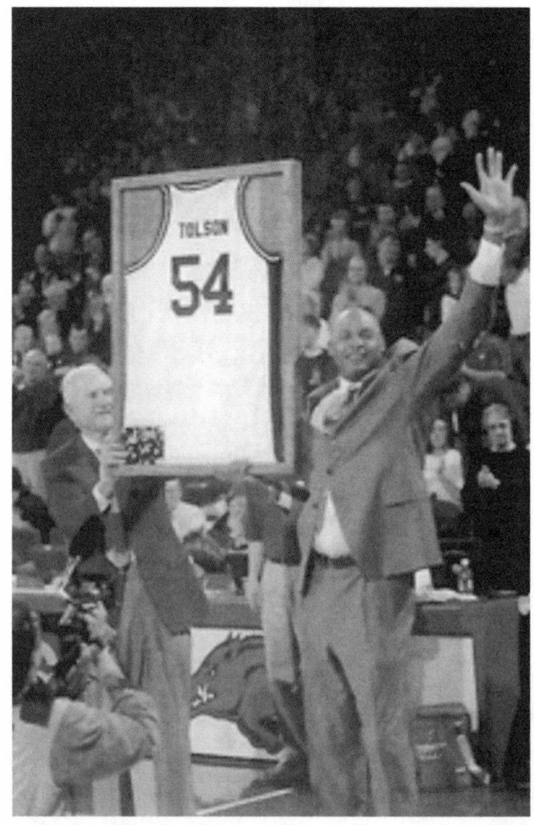

With Frank Broyles at my jersey retirement
COURTESY OF THE AUTHOR

Arkansas to give them the opportunity to come back and earn a college degree.

No honor ever had, or ever could, make me more proud or humble me more. My heart overflowed beyond words.

My number was retired, and my jersey was hung from the rafters of the Bud Walton Arena in a ceremony in front of a sold-out crowd. That same crowd leapt to their feet and cheered when Coach Broyles and I presented the first Dean Tolson Comeback Scholarship Award.

Graduation week in May was almost—*almost*—an anticlimax.

I still chuckle when I remember the guy who took my measurements for my graduation gown and said, "It's going to take a whole roll of material to cover you up."

The Arkansas weather was even warmer than usual for that time of year as friends and family arrived for the ceremony.

My nephew Brandon Tolson, my oldest brother's son, and my oldest brother's wife Renee drove in from Dallas. My younger brother's son, Brenton Lee Tolson, came from Kansas City with my sister Boni. My pal and Venezuelan teammate Larry Spicer showed up from Memphis.

And of course, the superstar of the group, my biggest fan of all, the reason I existed and the reason I'd overcome illiteracy and gone back to college in the first place, my mother, my hero, was there, beaming like she was lit from the inside.

The day before the ceremony, Mother cooked all of our family favorites—fried chicken, catfish, collard greens, potato salad, and those fluffy bread rolls she made that you had to eat fast before they floated off the plate. I went outside my apartment where we all gathered, and we fired up my barbecue grill to cook ribs, hamburgers, and hot dogs. I cooked for my brothers and sister, just like the old days. We laughed and told stories with such love and contagious joy I can't find the words to describe it.

The next day, I rented a limousine to take family, friends, and me to breakfast, the graduation ceremony and the after-party. After an hour or so at IHOP of more reminiscing about my early days as a basketball player, how high I could jump, my dunking skills, and some good-natured teasing about a few of my "bloopers" on the court, we joined a packed house of 22,000 people at the Bud Walton Arena. Once we were seated,

I peeked into a package with my name on it from the university that was waiting beside me. I couldn't wait to see my diploma! Instead, there was nothing but a bunch of formal letters and signatures. No diploma. Which goes to show how nervous I was, imagining I'd find my diploma beside my chair, all set for me to grab and run! But no, after all we graduates had been through to get there that day, it made sense that they'd want to honor us with something a little more formal.

In the million years or so I sat there waiting for the announcer to finally get around to the Ts in the alphabetical lineup, I couldn't help but think of the people who hadn't believed in me—the Bill Russells and the Lenny Wilkenses of the world; the teachers and professors who thought I was just another dumb ballplayer—and wishing they could see me now.

And naturally, my mind drifted to questions about the next chapter in my life, and the incredible realization that, at age 57, my life was just beginning.

Finally I heard the announcer say, "Tolson."

I walked across the stage, memorizing every image around me—the bright lights, the flower arrangements, the members of the Board of Governors Committee standing there to shake my hand and say, "Congratulations, Dean." I managed to catch a glimpse of my people in the audience: my family, my friends and many acquaintances, Coach Broyles, Marcia, Great Scott, all of them on their feet applauding me, all of them deserving to be right up on that stage with me. I struggled to take it in so I could replay it over and over for the rest of my days, aware with every step I took that *this moment would never happen again.*

When I got to the end of the stage, I was handed that iconic scroll with red ribbon around it. I slipped off the ribbon to read my diploma on my way back to my seat. I had a flash of that bad dream I'd had about the president of the university snatching back my undergraduate diploma when I reached for it, and I needed to see this to make sure it was real.

Of course, the joke was on me. I learned later that the actual diploma would be mailed to my home in Tacoma. No problem, as long as I got it and could actually hold it in my hand. Maybe then I'd believe this really happened.

Once all the festivities were over, Coach Broyles called me into his office and told me he was getting me a job with the University of Arkansas.

Sadly, it would never happen. The writing was on the wall that Frank Broyles's power at the university was diminishing. He'd already announced that he was resigning as the U of A athletic director at the end of 2007 to become athletic director emeritus of the Razorback Foundation—pretty much an honorary title, because the university was firing him.

Coach Broyles had raised over a billion dollars for the school, most of which went to the athletic department, and none of which mattered to the school anymore. It was all about hiring someone who could raise the *next* billion dollars for them. But with Coach Broyles, my biggest advocate, leaving the University of Arkansas, he'd be taking any opportunity I had to work there right along with him.

Needless to say, I empathized. I knew exactly how it felt to go from "big deal" to "never heard of you," even if you'd been successful and put your heart and soul into your career.

And it was that empathy, and those thoughts in general, that helped the purpose of the final act of my life come into focus, once I managed to exorcise the one last demon that could destroy me if I let it.

Chapter Nineteen

Ceremonies, accolades, and excitement behind me; my jersey retired; scholarship in my name initiated; *magna cum laude* master's degree secured . . . I returned home to Tacoma broke and broken.

My back pain was excruciating and relentless, and it was crushing my soul. I wanted desperately to get off my painkillers once and for all, but I'd learned the hard way that trying to detox myself was a *really* bad idea, and lying on my living room floor unable to move for the rest of my life was out of the question. I could feel myself dying every day.

But as fate would have it, the union of retired NBA players had started doing some outreach to their members on health issues, so I managed to get to the National Basketball Retired Players Association convention in Las Vegas. While I was at the convention I was connected with one of the union's partners, an organization called PAST (Pain Alternatives, Solutions and Treatment). They had a program to help me get clean from painkillers, but first they wanted to address what was causing the pain in the first place.

Thanks to PAST and the retired NBA players union, I made several trips to New Jersey for diagnostic exams and surgical procedures. They gave me epidural injections for my back, and the needles were so painful they had to anesthetize me just to administer the shots. When those injections weren't effective, they gave me two facet injections that offered pain relief for up to a few months. They finally repaired the torn ACL in my right knee from that basketball injury in Venezuela over two decades earlier, and they even opened me up to fix the umbilical hernia that had caused my intestines to stick out an inch and a half through my navel.

By the time they were done trying to mend my body, they'd administered over $200,000 worth of medical treatments. The rest of my $250,000 limit was going toward sending me to Behavioral Health of the Palm Beaches, a drug rehabilitation clinic.

For 40 days and 40 nights, their staff helped detox my body from a decade of opiates. My "clinic-mates" were mostly kids in their 20s, whose parents had dropped them off, written a $40,000 check, and told the clinic, "Send them home when you're done. I can't help them anymore."

Between being bored and wanting to use again, those kids acted out a lot. Sometimes they'd come to my room and talk to me, and most of them would eventually ask, "Dean, why is this so easy for you? Why are you so calm?"

It was simple for me. I didn't want to use drugs. I never had, and I never would. I wasn't taking drugs because it was fun, I was taking them to survive. And now that the doctors in New Jersey had repaired some of the injuries I'd been dealing with for years, what pain I still felt was tolerable enough to begin living my life again. I was starting to get my strength back, and I enjoyed talking to those kids and trying to encourage them.

"You're still young! You still have your whole lives ahead of you! I'm almost 60, and I just got my master's degree. Imagine what you can do with the next 40 years of your lives!"

It fit in so perfectly with the plan that was taking shape in my mind when I walked out of rehab clean and sober.

I finished the program, went back to Tacoma, and made the big decision to move to Scottsdale, Arizona, where I still live to this day. It was exactly the right thing for me to do. The warmer, drier weather allowed me to take walks outside all year round to maintain and improve my health. My body was getting less and less painful by the day, my mind was getting clear and loved being drug-free, and I felt alive again. And I began to not just know but understand what I wanted to do with my life.

I wanted people to stop dying and start living.

I wanted younger people to find a worthwhile purpose in their lives and get an education to help them get there.

I wanted people to realize, much earlier than I did, the impact their lives can have on the lives of those closest to them, or even casual observers. As I get older, I think about that a lot.

What if Wilt Chamberlain had never come to my house that day in Kansas City and been such a great guy?

What if Warren Jabali, who was a big deal basketball star, had never stopped to talk to me on the street when I was in high school and taken the time to become my friend and encourage me to pursue my dream?

What if a businessman like John McDaniel had never called me out of the blue to come talk to students and stuck around to become my mentor?

What if losing that million-dollar Boeing contract because I was making more than the plant manager had bankrupted me and sent me into financial despair that could have led me to a premature death?

What if I had resisted arrest that early morning in Tacoma, Washington, and compelled the police to shoot and kill this 6-foot-9 Black man who made them feel "threatened for their safety"?

What if my mother had said, "Sure, go back to Greece and play basketball," instead of begging me to go back to school and learn to read and write?

What if Frank Broyles hadn't believed in me enough to put me on scholarship again at the University of Arkansas and reduced me to being just another statistic of a collegiate system that makes millions off of athletes and then discards them when they don't serve a purpose?

What if Marcia Hariell and Great Scott had dismissed me as not worth the effort?

What if . . . so many people and choices I can't even count them all?

And then there's the honor of being someone else's "what if?"

When I went back to Arkansas to get my undergraduate degree, it gave my older brother the courage to go back to school. He got his GED and went on to earn his undergraduate degree and an MBA.

My sister Boni was inspired to complete her education as well. She had a basketball scholarship to Sterling College as an undergraduate and

Holding diploma with principal at South Kitsap High School in Bremerton, Washington.
COURTESY OF THE AUTHOR

Addressing student body at South Kitsap High School in Bremerton, Washington
COURTESY OF THE AUTHOR

went on to earn two master's degrees and a doctorate from the University of Hawaii—the first person in our family to earn a doctoral degree.

In other words, three out of five Tolson kids raised by a single, struggling mother in the Kansas City ghetto, and, temporarily, by an orphanage and a foster home, eventually came away with master's degrees and a PhD. All because when they saw that I could do it, the least likely of all of us to succeed academically, they realized that they could do it too.

It's funny, the things you find yourself thinking about when you get older, when you're not young and immortal anymore. Taking my daily walks around quiet neighborhoods in Scottsdale, it would suddenly occur to me that I didn't want "former NBA player" to be the first line of my obituary. I wanted my legacy to be much greater than that. I wanted to be remembered as someone who helped the people of this world, no matter what their age or their circumstances along the way, not to give up until they find a better life, and a purpose that makes them proud. To be someone else's "what if?."

Today my motto is very simple. "Each One Teach One."

Which is why, for more than 30 years now, I've been a public speaker and mentor for people of all ages.

I speak about education. How I totally dismissed it when I was young because it seemed like something other people wanted me to do that interfered with what *I* wanted to do, and how, in the end, it led me to the best, most rewarding time of my life.

I speak about the importance of dreams. How I achieved mine, only to find myself discarded, broke and broken, and discovered that our lives aren't limited to just one dream after all.

And I speak about building the confidence and the courage to pursue those dreams.

Being a 6-foot-9 former NBA player helps get audience attention when my name is announced at speaking engagements. But what keeps that attention once they're in their seats is my hard-earned message that it's up to each of us to be the heroes of our own stories, especially at a time in today's world when so many feel lost.

We live in a society in which many people feel directionless. Feeling that life has no purpose leads to anxiety, depression, and bad decisions. I've outlived the odds. I'm not supposed to be alive today to tell my story,

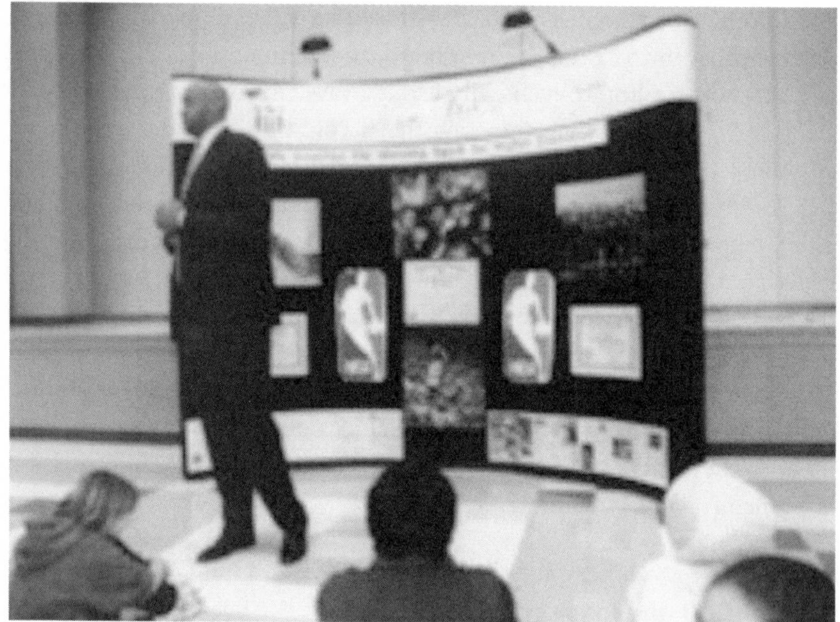

In front of a presentation backdrop at McNair Middle School in Fayetteville, Arkansas
COURTESY OF AUTHOR

and yet, I'm here—so apparently I *am* supposed to be alive today to tell my story. I can honestly say I cherish every day of this life. And as long as I'm breathing, I want to share some of the lessons I speak about, lessons I've learned that have helped me live and thrive and, I believe, can do the same for you.

It all starts with purpose.
You can memorize all the maps in the world, but it won't make a damned bit of difference if you have no idea where you want to go. I was very fortunate to know when I was nine years old that I wanted to play professional basketball. Invest the time to dig deep within yourself to think about what would make you happy, not just for a few days or weeks or months, but for life. It will change over time, so do this often. As I got older and my body refused to let me play basketball anymore, I had to find a new purpose. Once you think you know what you want to do

and achieve, the thing inside you that makes you happy, you now have a destination. Now you can make a map of how to reach that destination, because now you know where you are and where you're headed.

Make your dream a goal.

Goals are simply dreams that you write down and commit to achieving. People think that they set goals all the time—for example, every January, you usually hear someone say, "I made a New Year's resolution to lose weight." That's not a goal. A goal is something specific that you remind yourself of every day in order to make it a reality. Once you've written your goals down, look at them every day. Remind yourself what's important. Is what you're doing each day helping you reach your goal? Are your friends helping you reach your goal, or are they discouraging you from reaching it? Once you're focused on what you want to achieve, distractions become easier to identify and avoid. Having goals helps you focus on what is important and also reminds you what isn't.

Develop a strategy.

There's a reason why you've set a goal to achieve your purpose—it's because achieving your purpose in life is hard. If it were easy, you wouldn't need to set a goal. You'd wake up and do it without thinking about it. That's why achieving great things always requires a strategy for accomplishing it. Whether it was playing in the NBA, going back to college when I was illiterate, starting my own company, or even getting my master's degree at age 57, I would never have accomplished any of those things without a well-conceived plan that also allowed me to use every possible resource I had to reach it. This is also where having a good mentor comes into play. A mentor is someone who's already had the success you're trying to achieve. They know how you can reach your goal because they've probably already reached it and know how to get there. A good mentor will help you develop the strategy you need to succeed and avoid pitfalls along the way.

Make the commitment.

This may be the most important piece of advice I have to offer. If you've found your purpose, set your goals, and have a strategy to get there (with the help of a mentor), it's now up to you. Now you have to make the commitment with your mind, heart, body, and soul to reach those goals. Failure is no longer an option. That's the "secret sauce" to success.

When I set that goal at the age of nine to be an NBA player, I made the commitment. I played for hours every day. I was the first kid in the gym when the doors opened (often thanks to Uncle Raymond) and the last one to leave when the doors were locked up again. I played morning, noon, and night until I had the skills and the confidence I needed to play against the best players in the world.

The same was true when I went back to college at age 32. There were days when I studied for 20 hours, prioritizing finishing all my assignments over sleep. When I started my carpet-cleaning company, I worked on jobs into the early morning hours until every square foot of carpet was clean to the customer's satisfaction.

So many people quit on their dreams before they reach their destination. Life is going to give you a lot of off-ramps because the process of achieving your goals is painful at times, and no one wants to experience pain. Quitting is easy, because it feels good. The pain is over. You feel relieved. But that short-term relief will lead to regret and the long-term pain of living an unhappy life, knowing you let yourself down. I accomplished my goals many times. I was a poor, uneducated kid from Kansas City who survived poverty, street violence, racism, and so many other obstacles along the way. If I can do it, you can do it. But you have to commit to what you're doing.

Believe in yourself.

This is the hardest part of achieving success. We all experience self-doubt. Sometimes it comes from the outside, from the people and circumstances around us. Sometimes it comes from the inside, our own minds and deep-seated beliefs in what kind of lives we *really* think we deserve. When I was a boy and announced I was going to play in the NBA, no one believed me, not even my own mother, who loved me more than anyone else in the world. When you don't truly believe in yourself, that's when your commitment really starts to waver. Maybe I'm not smart enough. Maybe I'm not good enough. Maybe I'm not lucky enough. Maybe I don't deserve it. When you start to believe that negative dialogue in your mind, you almost will it to come true, like the age-old saying, "What I fear, I create." When you start to let that negativity become the loudest voice in your head, you have to drown it out with positive thoughts and small victories and climb your way back to the big victory you're looking for.

This was never more true than when I went back to college for my undergraduate degree. Every day felt like an insurmountable challenge. But I'd made a commitment to take small steps I knew I could manage. Sit in the front of every class, and never miss a single day. Never go to sleep at night until I've finished that day's assignments. Get to know all my professors. And don't leave school until I've graduated.

There were many days when I cried. I was frustrated. The bigger goal, the bigger victory, seemed too hard to achieve. Impossible. But every day that I did the things I'd committed to counted. Every time I went into that classroom and took a seat right up front, I was a step closer. Every time I read my assignments, no matter how hard they were, I was a step closer. I gave myself every opportunity to believe in myself. And with every step forward, my confidence grew. Every passing grade was more wind in my sails.

Don't let anyone tell you that you can't accomplish something. Believing is achieving.

Build a team to help you.

As a basketball player, I've always understood the importance of good teammates. And the value of good teammates extends far beyond the basketball court. We all need a team of reliable people to help us succeed. In school, it may be friends to help you study, and academic advisers to help you develop the skills you need for academic success. In business, it may be mentors to help you learn how to do your job more effectively to earn more money and build a solid reputation, and reliable employers and employees with the honesty, integrity, and work ethic to keep things successful and moving forward.

Remember, the importance of having a team is that the sum of all their experience is greater than yours. You can learn from their past mistakes and accomplishments. They'll help motivate you when things get tough. Sometimes they'll come through in the clutch because they have access to resources you don't have. Many kids and adults alike are ashamed to ask for help because they think it makes them look weak. But being a good teammate means relying on your teammates for help when you need it and being there for them when *they* need it. Your successes are their successes, and their successes are yours. Surround yourself with the wrong people and you'll get the wrong results. But if you build a good team, you'll achieve the success you're striving for, and it will be much easier to get there than if you'd done it alone.

Always keep learning.

One of the biggest mistakes I made in life—and I made more than my share—was not taking my education more seriously when I was the age of so many of the kids in my speaking engagement audiences. I was good at basketball, so I didn't think education was important, and I never had anyone help me get back on the right track. It was easier for schools to keep promoting me from one grade to the next, so long as I kept getting better at basketball.

Going back to Arkansas to get my degree was, without a doubt, my greatest accomplishment. I didn't win my championship in the NBA; I won it in the classroom. Having a good education is the solid foundation you need to find and achieve your purpose in life. I may have reached the NBA, but when it was time to find a new purpose, a new reason for living, I was unprepared.

No matter what your age, you need to keep feeding your mind in order to grow. If your mind isn't growing, it's dying. It's tough to realize this when you're younger. The road in front of you seems endless. But as you get older, the ride gets shorter and shorter when you let your mind wither. Even if you've finished your formal education, don't let your mind grow weak from neglect. We have more resources that allow us to learn than ever before. Being born on a poor Kansas farm, I never imagined having internet access to books I could check out and read from my own home. Always value and respect these amazing resources and take full advantage of them. Learning is a continuous investment that you make in your own happiness.

Pay it forward.

Every day I get to walk outside in the sunshine is a blessing, a gift. I'm very lucky to be alive and well and able to tell my story. And this has become my purpose in life, my legacy, to help others stay on the right track in life and fulfill their own dreams.

There was a time in my life when I was focused solely on basketball, then college, then my business, then my master's. My final purpose is one we should all have—to leave the world a better place than it was when we got here. If you'll just pay it forward and lend a helping hand to someone who needs it, you'll be part of the greatest legacy there is, and you'll truly be a success.

I made a promise to God at one of the low points in my life that if He would help me through it, I would do His work for the rest of my life. Each One, Teach One is His work.

The poet Robert Frost once wrote, "I have promises to keep, and miles to go before I sleep."

I'd be honored if you'd walk those miles with me.

Epilogue

It's not an easy thing to tell your life story. Though some moments still make me smile, or even laugh out loud, other moments inflicted wounds that remain fresh and raw. But hiding wounds doesn't help them heal, nor does it help anyone else learn from them, and in the end, the possibility of all of us healing and learning together makes the occasional pain of writing this book more than worth it.

I also think it's important for all of us who've survived to tell our stories, especially African Americans and other minorities who've had to deal with a lifetime of systemic racism, because the problems we've faced all our lives haven't gone away. During this global crisis of the coronavirus, countless athletes were asked to continue playing while sports fans were forbidden from attending and watched safely from home instead. It didn't matter that the health risks were taken mostly by minority athletes who were most vulnerable during the pandemic, and any message to anyone on this planet that they're more expendable because of their race diminishes us all, at a time when we've never needed each other more.

That is one of the main reasons I've decided to tell my story now, in the hope of illustrating that no matter what obstacles we face as life goes along, we have to keep moving forward and keep trying to grow. There are always going to be twists and turns in whatever road we choose to travel, but it's never too late to get back on that road when we make wrong turns and think we're hopelessly lost.

This isn't just my story; it's also my mother's story. She passed away in 2010, and my heart will always be full of the love she gave so fiercely to her children and grandchildren, even during those rough times when love was all she had to give us. It's strange to keep walking ahead when you can't see your biggest fan and your biggest supporter walking beside you, but I'll always feel her and hear her guiding me in those quiet moments when I slow down, get out of my own way, and take the time to listen. This book is as much about her as it is about me.

This book is also about everybody who has a dream. Whether you're fortunate enough to make that dream come true or you fall short, dare to dream again. It's never too late. Every night you close your eyes is an opportunity to dream. And every morning that you open your eyes again is another opportunity to make that dream come true.

A Letter to My Mother

Dear Mother,

Thank you for being the devoted mother who diverted my attention away from the game of basketball, which I loved so much with all my heart and soul. You convinced me to go back to college and graduate from the University of Arkansas with honors, *magna cum laude*. What a journey!!!

It was you who hid from me my passport, basketball contract, and plane ticket in our Kansas City home. You got my undivided attention, which changed my focus and convinced me to stop playing the game of basketball. You changed my attitude to working toward a higher level in my life. You were the only person on earth who could persuade me to retire from playing, go back to school, overcome illiteracy, and graduate. As a child growing up, I always minded you and tried to do whatever you asked me to.

The steadfast conviction and love you had for me overpowered any game I could have ever participated in. Mother, your understanding of the dynamics and logistics of life were right on point, when I could not see it for myself at the young age of 32. You brought it to my attention and made it so crystal clear that one day I'd grow old and never play basketball again.

Out of the millions and millions of high school, college, and professional athletes in American history, your son can now proudly claim, I am the first illiterate athlete to ever go back to college, overcome illiteracy, and graduate with honors with a master's degree *magna cum laude*. I thank everyone along the way who believed in me and knew I could achieve this impossible dream.

Thank you, Mother
Love you, Love you, Love you
Your #2 son, Dean Tolson

Acknowledgments

"Better Your Best, and Bring Out the Best in Others."

That slogan, given to me by renowned author and public speaker Keith Harrell, lies at the core of the message I've been privileged to share for the past 30 years, in live appearances for everyone from corporate America, to the American workforce, to at-risk students and student athletes and students who are simply feeling lost and discouraged, to professional athletes—anyone who's looking for the inspiration and motivation to keep learning and continuing their education. It was thanks to a cold-call from a man named John McDaniel, who invited me to speak to an assembly of 3,000 students at a Tacoma, Washington, high school, that I discovered the joy of making a meaningful difference by sharing my story, and it's that joy, that passion, that led me to finally write this book and tell my story to the rest of the world.

That I can even read a book, let alone write one, is a gift that still amazes me to this day, more than a decade after graduating with my master's degree, *magna cum laude*. I'm eternally indebted to the many people who refused to let me settle for being one hell of a basketball player . . . who also happened to be illiterate and hopeless when his days on the court were over with:

My mother, Melba Tolson, the most influential person in my life, the woman who gave me the most painful, loving kick in the butt exactly when I needed it; Marcia Harrell, my "God-send tutor," the person who not only opened her brilliant mind and her home to me but also brought out educational skills in me I didn't even know I possessed and taught me how to learn; The University of Arkansas Razorback Foundation, whose administrative leadership supported me, financially and academically, through some of the biggest challenges I'd ever faced; and standing head and shoulders above all the rest, Coach Frank Broyles, head coach and athletic director at the University of Arkansas. It was his leadership and guidance that formed the backbone of my decision to continue my education and ultimately graduate. "You can do this, Tree," he said, and because I believed him, I have firsthand knowledge of how it feels to proudly promote the importance of getting a quality education. Coach Broyles was my first real father figure, the man who showed me that I was much more than who I thought I was, the man who went through this odyssey with me, side by side every step of the way, and brought out the best in me. He loved me, and he proved it in so many ways, including giving me credit for bringing a whole new style of basketball to the University of Arkansas campus, a style that prompted the team to become known as "The Runnin' Razorbacks."

Coach Frank Broyles is the best friend I ever had in my life, and even though he left this world in 2017, I don't just believe, I *know* he can hear me when I say, "You made this book possible, Coach. I thank you for that, and for everything else, and from the bottom of my heart, I love you too."

A Postscript

I also pay tribute to fellow players, coaches, and mentors who have passed on to the next life: Bill Russell (coach), Bob Hopkins (coach), Dennis Johnson (roommate), Lonnie Shelton, Marvin Webster, Paul Silas, John Johnson, John Brisker, Bruce Seals, Mahdi Abdul-Rahman, Willie Norwood, Larry McNeill, Bob "The Voice" Blackburn, Zollie Volchok, and Sam Schulman.

I spent two-and-a-half years writing this book. On Sunday, July 31, 2022, the day I put the final period at the end of the final sentence, the news hit that Bill Russell passed away. Rest in peace, Coach Russell.